GW01239672

The Suffolk Golding Mission

A Considerable Service

Roy V Martin

Brook House Books

First published in Great Britain in 2014 by Brook House Books

ISBN 978-0-9557441-7-4

A considerable service has been rendered to the Allied cause by the safe arrival of this shipload.

The last sentence of Herbert Morrison's speech to the House of Commons, when in Secret Session, on 27 June 1940

Contents

Acknowledgements

Many people have helped me with information and advice while this book was in preparation. Family members of those involved include: Dr Don Cody (Olaf Paulsen's grandson), Ian Golding and the Hon Maurice Howard. Bruno Comer is preparing Paul Timbal's extensive account of the trip for publication, he has helped me enormously. Matt Hilton, has provided information about Bordeaux and was the first to come up with the 'writer' connection. I have received help from many on the WW2 Talk Forum, particularly Andy (DREW5233) and Lee Richards (PsyWar), Both provide an excellent, and economical, copying service for documents at The National Archives and elsewhere. The Operation Aerial record was provided by Don Kindell; Don has been very ill, I wish him a speedy recovery.

I struggled to explain the use of heavy water as a moderator and had to admit to myself that I didn't begin to understand the science behind it. My wife's cousin, Terence Holland, spent most of his working life in the nuclear world; he came up with the explanation within twenty four hours of my cry for help.

Special thanks are due to Hamish Roberts, a fellow Master Mariner, who is also a Barrister and the Archivist of Southampton Master Mariner's Club. I asked Captain Roberts if he would proof read the MS; he did much more, effectively becoming my Editor.

That said I accept full responsibility for any errors.

Author's Note

I first chanced upon this story while gathering material for *Ebb and Flow, Evacuations and Landings by Merchant Ships in World War Two.* After the book was published I started to read about the Earl of Suffolk and his journey. Most of the early stories I read seemed like fiction, which they largely were. Then I found the relevant files in The National Archives at Kew and learnt that this was in fact The Suffolk Golding Mission. With a great deal of help from those acknowledged above, I was able to flesh out the story.

Ebb and Flow was republished as *Merchant Ships in Action, Evacuations and Landings in the Second World War* and I was able to put more of the story in that book. Since then more material has come to light and I realised that this was a most interesting story in its own right. The publisher of the second book claimed 'Copyright © in introduction', so I have had to rewrite sections of my own work – this I have done to the best of my ability.

Don Kindell discovered the Operation Aerial journal. I transcribed it so that it was searchable and sent a copy back to Don. With my agreement it is now on the Naval History website in the Section on Admiralty War Diaries of World War Two.

The photographs that I have included do not meet the printer's standards. I have kept them in because I feel that they are relevant to the narrative.

I have made every effort to get in touch with copyright holders and apologise if I have unintentionally infringed any copyright.

Roy Martin, July 2014.   www.brookhousebooks.co.uk.

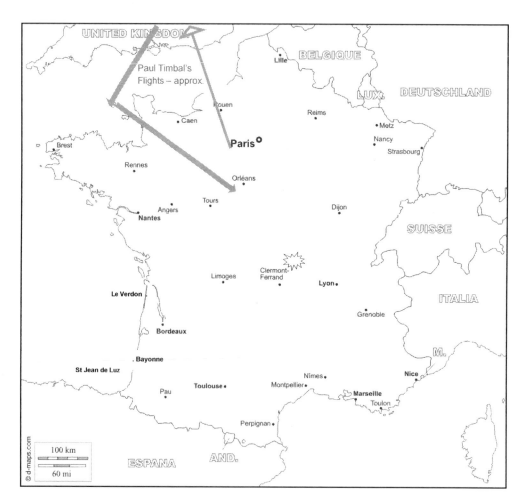

http://d-maps.com/m/europa/france/france/france26.gif (with additions)

Escape

Denholm's tramp steamer *Broompark* arrived in Bordeaux on 13 June with a cargo of Tyne coal. Paris was occupied on the next day. The *Earlspark*, another Denholm ship had also loaded coal in the Tyne; but was torpedoed and sunk while in convoy with the *Broompark*.

After discharging her cargo the *Broompark's* Master was asked if he was willing to embark five hundred refugees. He agreed, even though his ship had only the most basic of amenities. As it was the *Broompark* was only called upon to load just over one hundred passengers, but some brought with them cargo of immeasurable value to British in their forthcoming isolation. The ship sailed from Bordeaux at 0600 19 June 1940, making the trip down the Gironde without a pilot or tugs.

As he took his ship out into the estuary Captain Olaf Paulsen could have been forgiven for reflecting on how the war had changed his fortunes. In 1938 Denholm had made him redundant for grounding one of their ships, though they said that he had decided to retire. Unlikely, as the Merchant Navy pension scheme had only been going from 1 January of that year. He was now in command of their newest ship, with probably the most valuable cargo that they had ever carried. In addition he carried passengers who would have normally only be seen on the first class promenade deck of an ocean liner.

Paulsen had been born in Christiania, now Oslo, in 1878. He had made his home in Scotland and became a British citizen in 1904. His Master's Certificate qualified him to command a British merchant ship; with it he joined the Denholm Line of Glasgow. There he gained a reputation for being exceeding careful with the company's money; it was not easy to stand out in this way in a tramp ship company and a Scots one at that.

In the only photograph the ship already appears to be shabby, with her hull painted with hastily mixed grey paint. She proudly declares her identity by flying her signal letters and the biggest Red Ensign she has. The ensign flies where the gaff would have been on a grander ship, probably because the ensign staff had been taken down as it interfered with the scope of the, newly fitted, stern gun.

The Gironde estuary runs north-west from Bordeaux and Paulsen and his officers would have been well aware that the invading Germans would be likely to arrive first on the northern shore.

Looking down on the decks Paulsen could see that many of the men were already about. They had had to sleep, as best they could, either on the hatches, or in the tween deck; while the women and children slept in cabins vacated by the ship's officers. Most of the men already looked like coal miners emerging after a shift, but in collars and ties.

An almost piratical figure with several days' growth of beard seemed to be the centre of attention. This was 'Wild Jack' Howard or to give him his full title: Charles Henry George Howard, 20th Earl of Suffolk and 13th Earl of Berkshire, BSc (Hons.), F.R.S.E. He was dressed in a grubby greatcoat and walked with the help of a stick. The coat would be taken off as the day warmed up, to reveal a pair of pistols in shoulder holsters and tattoos that only sailors acquired in those days. At seventeen Jack had served for over a year as an apprentice on one of the last of the square rigged sailing ships, only leaving when the windjammer was sold for scrap. Then, after a short spell as an Army officer, Jack signed on a steam ship and migrated to Australia, where he farmed for some years.

The man with him, Major Ardale Vautier Golding, wore the uniform of an officer in the Royal Tank Regiment. Though he had made the same perilous journey across France; Major Golding was shaven and smart. At thirty seven he was three years older than the Earl; he had gained his BSc, in Mechanical Engineering, at the University of London. After graduating he had joined the Army, where his record shows that he was frequently 'specially employed'. Major Golding was in fact a member of Military Intelligence.

With their secretaries, Eileen Beryl Morden and Marguerite Nicolle, they had formed a mission to Paris, only leaving when it became an 'open city' on the 10 June. Now they were supervising the safe stowage of the valuable records they had saved. They had also organised the evacuation of most of the French scientists, many with their families, who were on the *Broompark*.

In declaring Paris to be an 'open city' the French abandoned all efforts to defend it. By doing this they expected the Germans not to attack, but simply march in, which they did. The French excused this as an attempt to protect the historic city and its population.

Two others on the deck were the bulky Lew Kowarski and Hans van Halban. They had brought with them the 187 kilos of heavy water (deuterium oxide) that agents of the French Secret Service had smuggled out of Norway. It had first been sent to the *Collège de France* laboratory of the French physicist Jean Frédéric Joliot-Curie. When the Germans invaded Joliot-Curie had instructed his colleagues to get the heavy water to Britain, where they were to continue their work. This consignment of the nuclear moderator was all that existed in the world.

Lew Kowarski was born in St. Petersburg in 1907; his father was the Polish -Jewish businessman Nicholas Kowarski and his mother the Ukrainian singer Olga Vlassenko. When he was 12 years old the Kowarski family fled west and settled in Vilnius (then in Poland). Young Lew was a talented musician, but his fingers grew too large for the piano keyboard. In 1934 he joined Joliot-Curie's group after gaining a degree in Chemical Engineering and a PhD.

Hans von Halban was born in Leipzig in 1908. His father was also of Polish-Jewish descent and his mother's family came from Bohemia. His grandfather, Heinrich Blumenstock, who had been a senior official in the Habsburg Empire, moved from Kraków to Vienna in the 1850s. Hans Halban was educated in Leipzig and Zurich. He joined Joliot-Curie's group in 1937, coming from the Copenhagen laboratory of the nuclear physicist Niels Bohr. Halban and Kowarski both became French citizens.

Also on the deck was a Belgian banker, Paul Timbal. Timbal was the Managing Director of the *Banque Diamantaire Anversoise*, the Antwerp Diamond Bank. He, and a representative of the Belgian government, had saved two crates of gem diamonds which they had transported first to Brussels and then across France. The diamonds had been deposited with the bank, each merchant having placed them in sealed envelopes. Timbal believed the total value to be between one and three million pounds sterling.

Timbal first took the diamonds to Paris, where they were deposited with the *Bank Transatlantique*; on 20 May the bank arranged for them to be moved to their facility in Cognac. On 8 June the RAF had flown Timbal to an airfield to the west of London, to meet Sir Ernest Oppenheimer, the Chairman of De Beers. It was agreed that the diamonds should be brought to Britain for the duration of the war. The diamonds were stored in a small cabin next to the Master's accommodation with the deuterium oxide, a sentry guarded the door.

In addition there were thirty three French scientists and technicians on board, many with their families.

The ship reached Le Verdon just before noon. There they loaded ammunition for the guns. They also hoped that some of the *diamantaires* from Royan could be embarked.

As the anchored ships turned with the changing tide the French passenger ship *Mexique* exploded and sank nearby. *Mexique* was there to embark French parliamentarians and take them to the French dependencies in North Africa. The shocked passengers now realised the hazards of the voyage. It was decided that the ship should delay no longer. Timbal said he watched the receding coast with a heavy heart, as he had also promised Oppenheimer that he would bring these diamond cutters to the UK.

The voyage home was relatively uneventful. The Master was as economical with words as he was with everything else; he does not record loading the cargo, or the passengers, but does say in an Official Log entry that with 101 souls on board he decided not to respond to a distress call from a ship with the signal letters ONVJ. This was probably the Belgian *Ville de Namur*, ninety miles away. The U-boat commander had suspected that this vessel was a Q-ship, because she had wooden structures on deck. These were stables for some of the nine hundred horses that the vessel had brought from Canada. All drowned, as did a number of the crew, in what must have been a terrible scene.

Morse light signals were seen astern, these were presumed to be from two U-boats who were following a nearby convoy, though they could have been from the convoy escorts. The seas were full of British and Allied merchant ships, who, during the three weeks that followed Dunkirk, evacuated almost a quarter of a million troops and civilians from France. Many of the ships were overloaded. Another open shelter deck tramp ship, the *Alderpool,* carried 3,526 Polish troops and civilians to safety. This ship ran out of food and drinking water. Her Master was one of a number who were awarded the Polish Cross of Valour and an OBE.

On the *Broompark* a raft was built to house both the diamonds and the heavy water; the idea of this 'ark' was that it would float if the ship sank. Timbal says how handy the Earl was, squarely hammering in the longest nails to make the raft. Suffolk and Golding dictated a document to Marguerite Nicolle setting out the precautions that had been taken to ensure the survival of the most precious items. Only a

French version is at the National Archives; this may be because French was the common language. Kowarski and, maybe others, could not speak English. The paper was signed by those in charge of the heavy water and the diamonds.

Some have suggested that the wooden structure on the port side deck of the *Broompark*, just forward of the bridge, was the raft. This is unlikely as the photograph was said to have been taken while the ship was in the Gironde, before the raft was built. There is a similar structure on the after deck, which gives rise to a more prosaic explanation – these were temporary lavatories erected ready for the five hundred who had been expected!

The *Broompark* went to action stations after aircraft had attacked the convoy, which was now about thirty miles away (see *Chorzow* in the chapter Other Rescues). The passengers were herded below into the tween deck. It was safer among the coal dust than on the exposed upper deck, but had the ship been torpedoed most would have drowned. Paul Timbal describes this raid, saying, among many other things:

> We were going full steam, straight at the enemy (?), the British flag flying proudly. I will never forget the Captain, a Scotchman, who stood bareheaded on his bridge, quietly smoking a pipe. ... The Captain, leaning against the bridge, continued to smoke his pipe calmly, his bronzed face of an old seaman was lit by the setting sun, towards which we were heading in a straight line.

Kowarski said the Earl was limping around the ship providing the seasick with champagne, which he said was the best treatment for the condition. Though the passengers only had enamel mugs to drink it out of. This intrigued Kowarski who felt that this action was in keeping with a P. G. Woodhouse character; but Jack Howard was no Bertie Wooster, in need of a Jeeves to keep him on track.

They arrived at Falmouth at 0630 on 21 June. Timbal recalled:

> We were in the middle of a bay and in front of us, in the bright sunlight, were green meadows and friendly houses. I couldn't restrain my emotion and almost shouted to my family. "We have arrived in England; our journey is ended!"

> I hurried on deck. Everyone was still asleep. Only a few passengers realized that we had arrived safely at our destination. Those who had been in charge of our lives, and had slept very little, were now sleeping, their duty accomplished. We were in a large bay, about half a mile from the coast which spread around us. ….All around us were merchant boats and yachts at anchor. Here, too, I noticed Dutch flags. A few warships, but of light tonnage. The chimneys of two sunken ships reached out of the water. Were these the results of a bombardment? … I did not know.

The harbour was crowded with ships, on one day there were ninety seven ships in the river Fal. There were liners, like the *Madura*, cargo ships and even Breton fishing vessels. The little boats from Brittany were retracing voyage made by their forebears more than one thousand five hundred years before.

PROCÈS-VERBAL

1°) Monsieur Paul J. TIMBAL, Administrateur Délégué de la Banque Diamantaire Anversoise, Chargé de Mission par le Gouvernement Belge et par le Ministry of Economical Warfare; Monsieur André J.L. Van Campenhout, Docteur en droit, Avocat à la Cour d'appel à Bruxelles, Chargé de Mission et Conseiller Juridique au Cabinet du Premier Ministre de Belgique, d'une part, chargé tous deux, en ses qualités, de transporter à Londres deux caisses deux plis scellés contenant des matières précieuses appartenant à la Banque Diamantaire Anversoise.

2°) Monsieur Hans H. Von Halben, chargé de Recherche de la Caisse Nationale de Recherches Scientifiques, collaborateur de M. le Professeur F. Joliot-Curie et Monsieur Léon Kowarski, Boursier de la Caisse Nationale de Recherches Scientifiques, d'autre part, chargé tous deux de transporter ensemble à Londres certains articles précieux provenant du laboratoire de Monsieur Joliot-Curie.

Considérant qu'ils ont pris place, avec les biens qu'ils transportent, à bord du Steamer marchand "Broompark" sur les indications de l'Ambassade Britannique se trouvant à Bordeaux, en vue de se rendre de cette ville en Angleterre;

que ces biens ont été embarqués, vu l'urgence né des circonstances de guerre, sans les documents et formalités d'expédition usuelles;

Considérant que les biens transportés sur un navire occupé par une centaine d'émigrants peuvent courir le risque de vol ou de sabotage; mais que le risque réel le plus vraisemblable est celui qui découle des éventualités de guerre;

Que bien que les soussignés ne soient point responsables des conséquences d'évènement de cette sorte, la nature même de leur mission les oblige moralement à se prémunir contre eux dans toute la mesure possible;

Considérant qu'en enfermant ces biens dans une cabine ou dans un coffre la probabilité de les sauver en cas de naufrage est quasi-nulle, d'autant plus que le capitaine de bord ne peut mettre de canot de sauvetage à leur disposition.

Ont décidé, après s'être consulté entre-eux et sur l'avis conforme du Earl of Suffolk son Secrétaire et du Major A.V.Golding, R.S.B.;

1) de fixer les biens dont il s'agit sur un radeau construit avec les marges de précautions,

2) de mettre ce radeau dans un endroit peu fréquenté du pont protégé par une garde armée et disposés de manière à ce que le navire coulent les biens surnage et puissent être

9

éventuellement sauvés.

3) de ne pas couper les amarres maintenant le radeau au pont
du navire dans le cas où les circonstances du naufrage
éventuelle donnerait à penser que l'on puisse s'en
saisir.

Le présent document est destiné à constater ces décisions
résultants de la délibération de personnes qui se trouvent dans
une situation identique ainsi que le fait que les mesures de
précautions ont été prises, la garde armée prévue ayant été
accordée et organisé par le Major Golding.

Ce document est fait en quatre exemplaires pour servir
au survivants des soussignés dans l'hypothèse ou un accident les
priveraient d'un ou de plusieurs de leur compagnons.

Il n'a pas pour objet et ne peut avoir pour effet de
diminuer ou d'augmenter la responsabilité des signataires de
cet acte à l'égard de leurs cocontants ou des tiers, cette
responsabilité ne pouvant être déterminée que par législation
applicable, dans le cadre de la mission dont chacun des signataires a été chargé et qui n'est ici que nominalement indiqué
pour définir l'identié des soussignés. Ce document n'a donc
d'autre objet que de servir de témoignage des décisions et
effet fait qu'il constate à celui des signataires qui désireraient
s'en prévaloir.

Fait en mer à bord du s/s "Broompark" le vingt Juin, 1940,
en quatre exemplaires, une copie supplémentaire étant délivrée
à chacun des témoins.

Paul J. TIMBAL   A.J.L.Van Campenhout

Hans H. von HALBAN   Lew KOWARSKI

Les soussignés attestent de l'exactitude des décisions,
circonstances et faits constatés au présent procès-verbal.

The Rt.Hon.Earl of Suffolk and Berkshire

Major A.V.GOLDING

Special Agents

Early in 1940 Major Golding and Lord Suffolk, with their secretaries
Marguerite Nicolle and Eileen Beryl Morden, went to Paris on behalf
of the Ministry of Supply. We know that the Earl travelled in February
because of articles in the Australian press. His first report to the
Ministry of Supply was dated 28 February.

The secretaries had been chosen for their ability to produce accurate
work under pressure, even when faced with difficult technical terms.
The task of the Mission, as it became known, was to identify people
and items of value to the British war effort; if France fell they were to
evacuate both. Major Golding, though nominally an officer in the
Royal Tank Regiment, was a member of Military Intelligence (MI1?);
he had studied mechanical and military engineering and had attended
the Military College of Science. In 1938 he had made a visit to Berlin to
report on Hitler's Army.

Charles 'Wild Jack' Howard was the 20th Earl of Suffolk and 13th Earl
of Berkshire. His mother Margaret was the daughter of the American
businessman Levi Leiter. When his father was killed on active service
in 1917 eleven year old Jack acceded to the title. He entered the Royal
Naval College, Osborne, and then Radley College, but left to sign on
the merchant windjammer *Mount Stewart*. In one article the young
Earl is described as an Apprentice and in the other a Cadet. The
Mount Stewart's Articles of Agreement and Official Log are at the
Memorial University of Newfoundland.

When he returned his family arranged a commission in the Scots Guards; but he left after his superiors complained of his habit of 'stage door handle polishing' – to use his own words. He then worked his passage to Australia on a steamship, where he worked first as a farmhand and in a saw mill. He later became co-owner of a farm in Queensland, with Captain McColm the former Master of the *Mount Stewart*. In 1934 he returned to the UK and married the actress Mimi Forde-Pigott, whose stage name was Mimi Crawford.

In June 1935 he was admitted to the Westminster hospital with a serious illness. This may have been when he contracted rheumatoid arthritis; he suffered from the after effects for the rest of his life and walked with a stick. His new wife encouraged him to study at Edinburgh University, where he gained a first-class honours degree in pharmacology with chemistry in 1938 (?) and was elected a fellow of the Royal Society of Edinburgh. At the outbreak of war he was classed as 'medically unfit' because of his arthritis.

He was that rare combination of an academic, a practical man and a leader. Those who knew him remarked on his willingness to work extremely hard and his ability to mix with all classes. The Earl's colourful exploits become the talk of Paris, while Major Golding kept a much lower profile.

Most found Jack Howard a delightful man, as one of the Belgian team observed *'c'était un très chic type'*; but to the old guard in the French Government he became the personification of Perfidious Albion.

Quite a bit of Lord Suffolk's time seems to have been spent dealing with requests from Metropolitan Vickers Electrical. Dr Gough wrote to him on 18 April pointing this out and suggesting that he should concentrate on his duties for the Ministry of Supply. In his reply Suffolk agreed that he was in danger of becoming a 'sort of unofficial traveller for Metropolitan Vickers.'

There is only occasional correspondence between the two men. Suffolk dealt with various things: bombs, without explosives, that were made of sheet metal and could disintegrate at a controlled altitude spreading material over a wide area; crack detectors; arranging visits to Porton Down and differential analysis. Once back in the UK the detection of infrared radiation was an additional subject.

There is no correspondence with, or mention of, Major Golding until, in a telephone call to the Ministry of Supply on 20 May, the Earl said that 'he felt that Major Golding was making rather too much of the question of evacuation of staff. Paris is calm.' 'He therefore proposes to remain unless he has instructions from the Director of Scientific Research to the contrary.' As a military man Golding probably had a better feel for what was happening, and was concerned about the safety of the civilian members of the Mission, if the Germans arrived.

In a letter to The Sunday Times dated 27 March 1960, Colonel Golding wrote, again from Paris, 'We kept in close touch with one another there, and throughout the evacuation.'

The Paris section of file HS 7/5, 'Special Operations Executive: Histories and War Diaries: Registered Files. Histories 'D' section', makes no mention of Major Golding; though some pages have been retyped and redacted. In February 2014 the file HS 7/3 'D section: early history to September 1940' was 'in use.'

Major Golding and Miss Nicolle left Paris in the early hours of Monday 10 June 1940. Miss Nicolle's 'Notes on our Flight from France' is in Appendix Three. It is a reasonable assumption that Lord Suffolk and Miss Morden left at the same time.

In the notes she says they left by the Porte de Versailles about an hour or so before the arrival of the Germans. In this she seems to be mistaken, Major Golding probably decided to leave when he heard that Paris was to be declared an 'open city' so it would not be defended. Italy declared war on Britain and France on that day, but Paris was not occupied until 14 June.

They had collected luggage and canaries (!) belonging to a Miss Bruneau of the M.A. (Ministry of Armaments) and called for a Mrs Morrison. Their progress was slowed 'by military convoys, lorries and war material which seemed to go both ways.' When they reached the suburbs they were caught in an air raid. They drove on without lights in a mist that Nicolle was later told had been created by the Germans. At 3.30 a.m. on 11 June, with dawn breaking, they stopped; after about half an hour, attempting to sleep on the top of their luggage and office papers, they continued towards Orleans.

At daybreak refugees seemed to be everywhere and even though they were in a military car they found it necessary to take to side roads to make any progress. This proved to be a good move as they arrived in Orleans at 9 a.m., earlier than 'the others'. After refuelling at a military base they breakfasted on tea and *biscottes* at a hotel. While there they met a Mrs MacDonald of the Mechanised Transport Corps. Major Golding went to her aid as she had run out of petrol. They then set off towards Tours, where they arrived at 1.30 p.m. in beautiful sunshine. The French government was temporarily at Tours, as were the various embassies.

When there they ran into a Major Withington; while he and Golding talked, the women hunted around for something for them all to eat. They could only find sandwiches. After this they tried to make their way to the British Consulate. It took them half an hour to cross the bridge at Tours, when they managed they found that they had been given wrong directions and they had to cross the bridge again. Once at the Consulate they were able to arrange onward transport for Mrs Morrison, who aimed to reach England via St. Malo. Then they met up with Mrs MacDonald 'and her girls' and Major Golding and Mrs MacDonald managed to find two rooms for the women. Miss Bruneau went to her office, where she was reacquainted with her boss.

In the morning they met up at the *Hotel L'Univers*, the women had slept well, despite an air raid and a few nightmares. However Major Golding had spent the night in his car, and had not been able to find hot water to shave. After filling up with petrol at the M.T.C. they set off with a Mr Metcalfe to arrange his flight to the U.K. He had been shot down by the R.A.F., on a previous attempt and lost his luggage.

The RAF made up for their mistake by providing everyone with a very good lunch. During this part of their journey they had the first of several punctures.

After 5 p.m. they set off for Bourges, a journey of about three hours. By now Golding was too tired to drive, so they stopped to eat, but could not find accommodation. Major Golding asked if there was a chateau nearby. There was, and they made their way there. They rang the old fashioned bell and, after a conversation through a closed door, they were let in by a young woman and a monk. The travellers were tired and dirty, but did not feel that they looked 'too villainous', however the occupants of the chateau decided to contact the police. Afterwards they were given wine and biscuits. Miss Nicolle was given a bed for the night, while the Major made do with a mattress on the floor. They learnt that there were nuns and children from the Metz district also sheltering there.

In the morning, of 13 June, they were given breakfast. After thanking the Vicomtesse for their Wayfarer's Dole they set off for Le Mont-Dore, via Montluçon and Clermont-Ferrand. At 4.30 p.m. when they reached their destination it was very cold and raining hard. There they meet a Colonel Raguet who showed them to their quarters, and an office from where they made contact with Lord Suffolk, we don't know how. The next morning they worked in the office until 9 p.m. There were 'already funny rumours running around' and they had to fight to keep their car and get petrol coupons for a trip that Golding intended to make to Paris.

At 8.30 a.m. on 15 June Major Golding knocked at Miss Nicolle's door and said that Paris had fallen, so they were off to Bordeaux. When she reached the office a few minutes later she found that everyone had disappeared, then Lord Suffolk and Major Golding arrived and the car was reloaded. As they were finishing a crate arrived from Paris with their office files, they emptied these into a suit case, which they put into the car. It was 5 p.m. before they got away. They made their first stop at nearby Bourbouille, where they found that Lord Suffolk's car had been taken. They returned to Le Mont-Dore where Major Golding found a lorry, into which they loaded Earl's and Miss Morden's luggage. Then they all set off for Bordeaux, with a chauffeur driving Major Golding's car.

With Golding and the chauffeur Bloch sharing the driving they reached Bordeaux at about 2 a.m. on the morning of Sunday 16 June. An air raid was in progress and the town was blacked-out. They had difficulty finding the Prefecture, but when they did they took rooms in the nearby *Chapon Fin Hotel*, these had been reserved for a Minister and his secretary. It was 3 a.m. before they got to bed, and they were up again at 8.30. The secretaries were given the day off, providing they bought a large suitcase for the Earl. They met their bosses for lunch.

At six they returned to the hotel and at 7.30 their bosses returned with the news that they were to board a cargo ship that had recently discharged a cargo of coal. All their effects were loaded on to the lorry and taken to the *Broompark*.

Diamonds

M. Paul Timbal was the Managing Director of the *Banque Diamantaire Anversoise*, the Antwerp Diamond Bank. When the Germans threatened to invade his country on Friday 10 May the bank was overwhelmed with customers wishing to withdraw cash and deposit rough and partially cut gem diamonds as security. Timbal knew that his Jewish clients had much reason to fear the invaders, so he kept the bank open throughout Saturday. Withdrawals had to be limited to 50,000 Belgian Francs. Then Timbal decided to move the stones that were in his care to a place of greater safety. He was able to buy a decrepit lorry; which he loaded and escorted to Brussels, where the diamonds were deposited in the Belgian National Bank.

On 12 May it became obvious that the diamonds would need to be moved again and Timbal obtained permission to take the two crates to Paris, where they would be deposited with the *Banque Transatlantique*. Timbal wondered about his authority to take bank property out of the country; so it was decided that he should be accompanied by André Van Campenhout, legal advisor to the Belgian Prime Minister Pierlot. The two men set off in Timbal's Panhard car, with the crates in the dickey, both carried a pistol.

The weather was hot, and drinking water was often difficult to obtain. They drove along roads clogged by fleeing civilians, who were in every kind of transport and on foot. When darkness fell they were near Compiègne, there they stopped as driving with headlights was forbidden. The first question was the security of their precious cargo. By producing a letter that the French Ambassador had given them, they were able to persuade the local police to put the crates in a cell for the night. Then they managed to find a room in a nearby hotel.

The next morning they drove on to Paris, where, after a nervous trip through the unfamiliar streets, they found the bank and deposited the diamonds. The *Banque Transatlantique* transferred the diamonds to their establishment in Cognac on 20 May. Timbal could now devote time to the safety of his family, who were sheltering in Cannes. It was imperative that he moved them well away from the Italian border, as there were already fears that Mussolini would take advantage of the German success and invade France.

Cramming them all in the car he took his family to the comparative safety of a spa town near Béziers, where they had distant relations. On 18 May he bid them farewell and headed back to Paris. As a military reservist he was due to report for duty before 25 May, failure to do so would have meant the possibility of arrest.

On 25 May he was relieved of his duty to report for military service and was, from then on, able to give his whole attention to saving the diamonds and finding a suitable place to establish the industry for the duration of the war. By this time many of the *diamantaires* had been transferred to Charente, which he found to be as miserable and backward as Cognac, which he had also looked at. The French authorities tried to persuade him that the industry could be centred there, while the merchants could reside in the more salubrious seaside town of Royan.

Making his way to Royan he looked around the town, with the president of the *Diamant club*, Charles Van Antwerpen. Timbal was far from convinced that Royan would be suitable and news of the Belgian capitulation on 28 May did nothing to improve his frame of mind. Paul Reynaud's government now had a scapegoat, King Leopold III of the Belgians. Written in the dust on Timbal's car was *Sale Belge*, 'filthy Belgian'.

On 4 June the British consul general in Bordeaux had asked him to travel to London to discuss the future of the diamond industry. He returned to Paris to get permission for the trip from the Belgian authorities. Having obtained the necessary permissions he took off in an RAF aircraft from an emergency airstrip near Paris on 8 June. In London he met Sir Ernest Oppenheimer, the Chairman of De Beers, they discussed the possibility of moving the diamond industry to Britain.

On 13 June he was at the Air Ministry to take a flight back to France. While he was there Ernest Oppenheimer called to say that he had approval from all the necessary authorities to action what they had discussed. Oppenheimer authorised Timbal to officially advise the Belgian government of the British proposal. Then, with a number of British and Belgian officers, he was taken to an airfield to the west of London for the return flight.

With Paris about to fall they were diverted to a deserted airfield at Châteaudun, between Orléans and Le Mans. When they landed they had to go to the air raid shelter, leaving their luggage on the aircraft. After the raid the senior British officers were whisked away in a staff car; leaving Timbal, a Royal Navy Lieutenant and his orderly, and Major Renson of the Belgian Air Force to fend for themselves. More about the Lieutenant later; but why did a junior naval officer have an orderly and who was he?

They explained their predicament to a Turkish official who had arrived to take the return flight to London; he put his car at their disposal. In this they set off for Tours, again because the French government was there. They found that the road was jammed with fleeing refugees and had to abandon the car when it over heated.

On foot again they saw a French military lorry driving down the left hand side of the road in the direction of Tours. The Lieutenant stepped into the road and stopped the vehicle, which was driven by a French sailor with a Quartermaster (?). The Quartermaster made a place for him and his orderly to join him in the cab. However he said that there was no room for the other two. The Lieutenant insisted that they should be carried, so a tarpaulin at the back was lifted:

> To our great amazement, we found inside the truck four French sailors, dead drunk, lying on hundreds of bottles of champagne. They opened a bottle now and then, took a sip and then threw the bottle in the corner of the truck where it empties itself. Most of the champagne was Pommery-Grenot, 1928. There was also an ice box in the truck. Major Renson and I climbed in the truck amid the champagne bottles. The exhaust pipe of the truck must have been quite short, and the gas accumulated slowly inside the truck. Both Major Renson and I were nearly suffocated by the time we reached Tours.

Later he met the RNVR Lieutenant in New York, he was by then a Lieutenant Commander, from him Timbal heard that this was Admiral Darlan's champagne. When they boarded the *Broompark*, they found champagne being dispensed, this time by the Earl of Suffolk, as a cure for sea sickness. Was this also from the Admiral's cellar?

On arrival at Tours they were dropped at the *Hotel L'Univers*, while the transport went on to the British Embassy. Conditions in the Hotel were chaotic, with people sleeping in the passageways and the public rooms. Only by producing a twenty Franc note were they able to get a cheese sandwich and a bottle of wine.

They got up early on 14 June and spent much of the morning looking, unsuccessfully, for transport to Poitiers. As they talked in front of the Hotel an old Ford passed driven by two elderly Belgian reservists. After at first objecting the two men agreed to take them to Poitiers: they asked to be dropped at the Hotel de France, which the Belgian government was using for temporary offices. There Mr Timbal met a Mr Caes, *Chef de Cabinet au Ministère du Travail*. Timbal briefed the official on his trip to Britain and passed the message that he had received through Ernest Oppenheimer. He said that, though Caes congratulated him, he seemed disappointed.

When Paul Timbal and André Van Campenhout reached Bordeaux on the morning of Sunday 16 June they sought out the British Consulate. They found it close to the quayside, but it was closed and guarded, so they went in to a café in the same building. The wife of the patron was the concierge for Consulate and they persuaded her to allow them to use her staircase to bypass the guard – a prequel to *'Allo 'Allo*? Climbing the stairs from the café they found that several members of staff were at their desks, but no one would admit to knowing anything about them.

The Embassy people had arrived from Tours on the previous evening and were camped out in the building. Later the Lieutenant who had flown back to France with Timbal came in, with him were several sailors carrying equipment to set up a temporary radio station.

At the suggestion of Mr Evans from the British Embassy the Belgians made their way to the *Hotel Chapon Fin*, where they were to meet for lunch. They got in to the hotel, where they were surprised to see Admiral Darlan and his entourage arrive, laughing heartily (he obviously hadn't heard about his champagne!). Shortly thereafter the British Ambassador and his party arrived they were 'very dignified and very grave.'

When Mr Irving and Mr Evans came they were prevented from entering the hotel, which had been reserved for senior officials and ministers. France was about to fall, but rank was rank and the food in the *Chapon Fin* was the best in town. The four went elsewhere in search of a meal. After a hurried lunch they decided to head back to consult the Naval Control Officer, the improbably named Commander Cunard. Cunard agreed that the Belgians and their diamonds could be taken aboard a ship, but only if they got there by 1 pm on Monday. Timbal was told that he could not be offered transportation for his diamond cutters as the limited number of ships were to be reserved for British subjects, civilian and military.

Once the temporary radio station was working in the embassy the staff there would have received increasingly alarming news. One hundred and forty thousand members of the British Expeditionary Force had made their way westwards in the hope of rescue. In addition there were considerable numbers of allied troops and civilians to be evacuated to carry on the fight from the UK.

The British officials in Bordeaux had a great deal to worry about. No wonder Irving 'threw up his hands in a gesture of discouragement', all he could tell the persistent Belgian was that 'events were moving so fast in France that everything was in a state of chaos' and 'he could do nothing, neither could I.'

Back in Royan Mr Timbal was having no more luck with his own side. Mr Van Antwerpen was not passing messages, even though he had not refused to do so when asked. The strain of the previous few days caught up with Timbal and he lost his temper with Van Antwerpen; who made it very plain that, as President of the *Fédération des Bourses Diamantaires,* he was opposed to any plan to take the diamonds to England. In so doing he was questioning Timbal's authority to take them there of course.

By now it was 1.30 a.m. on Monday 17 June, the fate of Timbal's plan for the diamonds hung in the balance. He took what he believed to be the only course open to him. For the first time he outlined the gravity of the situation to them all: France was about to fall, an Armistice was in the offing and the diamonds would then be seized by the Germans. Until then only Van Campenhout and Van Antwerpen had been aware of the wretchedness of their situation. 'The two women present wept.'

Timbal then set about persuading them all of the necessity of moving the diamonds to the U.K. and outlined the permissions he had to do so. Mr Van Campenhout came out in support and Van Antwerpen appeared to go along with the majority. They then agreed on plans for Monday and, at nearly 3 a.m., an exhausted Timbal went to his bed.

On the Monday morning he left Royan while the others were still asleep. He arrived at the *Banque Transatlantique* in Cognac at 8 a.m., the bank was in a state of confusion and the manager was close to breaking down. M. Weyl was an elderly man who finally forced a smile and said 'Timbal, I am old, and I have had my time; these Germans will only get my old bones'.

Van Antwerpen did not arrive at the bank until 1030 and again he had failed to do as he had been asked – in this case to pick up a Mrs Williams, the wife of a bank executive, whose husband was in the U.K. Mr Weyl was also playing for time, something Timbal did not have. One of his excuses was that a Mr. De Haan had tried to have the export of the diamonds blocked on the grounds that there was an attempt to defraud French customs.

The two crates were finally released at 11.45 and put in Van Antwerpen's car; Mr Van Campenhout went with him as a representative of the Belgian government. Once he saw them off Timbal was then able to concentrate on fetching his family from Royan, where he arrived at 1215. When the Timbal family and their luggage were in the car they heard Marshall Petain's broadcast, saying that the war was over for France. On the journey to Bordeaux they were stopped frequently by the police and it was not until 6.30 p.m. that they arrived. Then with traffic at a standstill Timbal decided to walk to the Consulate -Embassy.

On the afternoon of 17 June the Embassy would have received the dreadful news of the sinking of the liner *Lancastria* and the loss of thousands of those who were on board.

When he arrived Timbal was able to see Commander Cunard, who told him that the diamonds and Van Campenhout were on the *Broompark*. Timbal then sat down to await the return of Mr Irving, increasing concerned for his family. When they arrived, at 9.30, Timbal took them to find something to eat. In the event all they got was stale bread and cheese. They returned to the Consulate and were told to come back early next morning. Friends of a friend put them up for the night. It was the twins' third birthday. That night there was an air raid.

Timbal walked to the Consulate early on the morning of Tuesday 18 June, it was 11 a.m. when Mr Irving arrived. He told the worried Belgian that the ship was still in port and gave him an embarkation ticket for the Timbal family and their nanny. Irving also did his best to contact the *diamantaires* in Royan. After going round the town, buying what little food was available, the Timbal family arrived alongside the *Broompark* shortly after noon.

Heavy Water

In March 1940 agents of the French *Deuxième Bureau*, led by a Lieutenant Allier, succeeded in smuggling 187 kg of heavy water (deuterium oxide – see Appendix One for a description of its use) out of Norway. The consignment was all that was stockpiled in Ryukan. In an agreement concluded on 9 March 1940 the stock was loaned to the French, free of charge. After the war they were to have the choice of purchasing the consignment, or replacing it.

Ryukan was later to be the scene of the film *The Heroes of Telemark*. Some sources say that the *Bureau* booked two or three flights to confuse the Germans; and that one of these, destined for Amsterdam, was intercepted and made to land at Hamburg. Allier and one other secret agent accompanied the first ten cans of the material on a flight to Scotland; the other sixteen cans followed two days later, accompanied by two more agents.

Another account says that the unpressurized aircraft flew so high that Allier passed out while stretched out across the cans of the precious liquid; when the pilot realised what had happened he hastily lost altitude and Allier regained consciousness.

The twenty six cans were passed to the *Collège de France* laboratory of the French physicist Jean Frédéric Joliot-Curie. Joliot-Curie and his wife Irène (Marie Skłodowska Curie's daughter) had shared the 1935 Nobel Prize for Chemistry. At the outbreak of World War II, Joliot-Curie was a professor at the *Collège* and it was there that the cans were stored in an air raid shelter.

When France was invaded Dautry, the French Armaments Minister, ordered that the consignment should be saved from the enemy. On 16 May a team from the Ministry, led by Allier, arrived at the laboratory. After a brief meeting it was decided that the heavy water should be moved away from Paris, together with a vast amount of other heavy material, including lead bars. Later in May Hans von Halban and a colleague moved south to Clermont-Ferrand, where they established a temporary laboratory.

On 6 June another colleague, Lew Kowarski, set off south with a convoy of trucks loaded with the bulk of the consignment, including the deuterium oxide. At Clermont-Ferrand they were met by Halban. The heavy water was put in a women's prison in the city of Riom. Lew Kowarski sent his wife and four year old daughter south by train. His daughter had been scalded some days before and her arm was in bandages. They were reunited at Clermont-Ferrand.

Allier arrived at the villa/laboratory on 16 June, in uniform. He, Joliot-Curie and Halban decided that Halban and Kowarski should leave for Bordeaux early next morning, with the heavy water. Joliot-Curie seems to have told Halban that he, Halban, would be responsible for the heavy water. This rankled with Kowarski, who considered that he was 'the heavy water man.' They set out in two cars. Halban had his wife and young daughter in one; Kowarski, who could not drive, was driven, again with wife and daughter. The journey must have been particularly uncomfortable for the burly Kowarski, who was lying on a few blankets laid across some twenty cans.

They drove throughout the day and did not reach Bordeaux until an hour before midnight 17 June. Once there they sought the temporary office of the Ministry of Armaments to receive their instructions.

Their orders were brief: they were to go to England in a ship that had been allocated to a Lord Suffolk, who had the use of it to evacuate scientists and material destined for Britain. There they were to put themselves, and the heavy water, at the disposal of the British authorities. They were to observe absolute secrecy. When in the UK, they refused to take orders coming from Colonel, later General, De Gaulle, as he was not a member of 'the British authorities'. This greatly annoyed the Free French leader.

Just after midnight 18 June the two nuclear scientists arrived at the ship with their families and the 'heavy water.'

The Broompark

Denholm had recalled the recently retired Captain Olaf Paulsen to take command of their newest ship, the *Broompark*. The ship had arrived in Bordeaux on 13 June, with a cargo of coal from the Tyne: she could carry about eight thousand tons, in bulk rather than in bags. Another of Denholm's ships, also laden with coal for Bordeaux, had been sunk while in the same convoy. On arrival Paulsen would have taken the ships papers to the British Consulate, where they would have been deposited while the ship remained in port. After the last of the cargo had been grabbed out of the five holds the Master returned to the consulate, he was told that Paris had fallen and refugees were streaming towards the western French ports in the hope of rescue.

The *Broompark* was an open shelter decked, coal fired, tramp steamer. She was only remarkable in one way; she had been launched on 12 September 1939, making her the first British cargo ship to be launched in the war. Her fitting out was a fairly simple matter and she was delivered to her owners, during the following month. She was the fourth ship to bear the name. The ship was 447 feet in overall length, with a beam of 56 feet. Her gross tonnage was 5,136 – this was a measure of the cubic capacity of her cargo carrying spaces, rather than a weight. When she arrived in Bordeaux the ship was still not fitted with defensive armament; but the French provided arms and gunners.

Tramp ships did not sail on a scheduled service, but normally went wherever cargoes offered. In the main they carried coal, ore, grain and sawn timber.

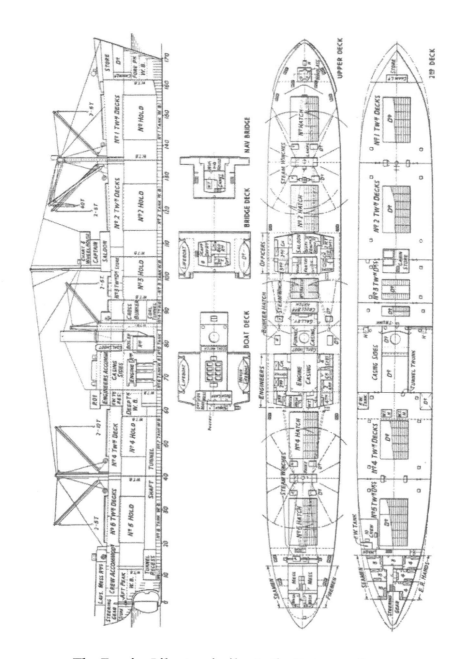

The Empire Liberty, similar to the Broompark.
Courtesy: American Bureau of Shipping (ABS)
This British hull design was used for the famous American Liberty ship

A shelter decker had one additional deck inside the hold, which ran the full length of the ship; this was about two feet above the load water line and was nominally the 'main deck.' Most tonnage measurement was made from this deck; to confuse everyone it was usually referred to as the 'tween deck.

The Navy was organising an operation, code named Aerial, to take as many British citizens as they could. Because naval ships were in short supply the burden would fall on the merchant ships, many of them simple cargo vessels like the *Broompark*.

Communications with his Glasgow office were impossible, so Paulsen had to make his own decisions. He agreed to take five hundred people and kept his ship in port until they could board.

On 16 June he again walked to the consulate, there he found a scene of confusion. The people from the Paris Embassy were there and it seemed as if thousands were camped in the street outside, all hoping to be evacuated. He was introduced to Mr Irving, the Commercial Attaché, who in turn introduced him to Major Golding and the Earl of Suffolk. The old shipmaster would have been more impressed with the fact that the Earl had been an Apprentice on the merchant square rigger *Mount Stewart*, than with his two titles. He was asked if he would take the members of the Mission, a number of scientists, with their families, and documents. This he agreed to do, assuming that they would be part of the five hundred.

The first members of the Mission boarded that night at 11.30 p.m. The secretaries together with Mdm. Berthiez, were shown to their temporary quarters on the ship, which was to be their home for nearly a week. The men returned to the *Hotel Chapon Fin*.

The women were told not to leave the ship, so they tried to rest; this proved impossible as they were 'all worked up.' There were rumours that France had capitulated. They retired to their bunks, after listening to 'the Captain's funny stories.' According to an article in a Denholm publication Captain Paulsen was:

> On the surface a quaint mixture of a showman and a clown, but underneath this masquerade lurked his true character which was one of intense drive and ruthless efficiency.

In the middle of the night they were told to get up as the port was being bombed. The ship seemed to be a target, possibly because of information passed by fifth columnists, so she was moved to another berth where loading and storing continued. This meant that Joliot-Curie could not find her, had he done so he would probably have been kept on board against his will.

Later Colonel Golding, as he had become, recalled:

> Quite by chance we discovered about 700 tons of recently delivered American heavy machine tools on railway wagons on the quay area. By arrangement with the Embassy, and helped by the French, we had them loaded on board, this took three days. … an employee of the Ministry of Aircraft Production arrived with two light lorries containing a few light machine tools.

The *Broompark* was unarmed so help was sought from the French to rectify this shortcoming. They provided three guns and gunners to man them. There is also a report of a team of R.A.F. men boarding for this purpose.

Miss Nicolle said 'stray passengers are beginning to come on board and I hear that it is the Captain's intention to take 500 refugees'. She decided that she needed to inform 'the bosses' about this. Both secretaries made their way to the British Consulate, where they found huge crowds outside waving their passports. Inside chaos reigned and their bosses are not there. They made their way to the hotel and from there to a restaurant without finding the men. Their car broke down, so they cadged a lift to the *Ministère de l'Armement*, where they tracked the two men down and told their tale.

At 4.30 p.m. they returned to the ship, where new passengers needed their attention. Those who counted as members of the Mission arrived expecting cabins, bunks and food. They were given blankets and told that only the women and children would be in cabins, the men had to sleep on the deck wherever they could find space. Loading continued in heavy rain.

Kowarski and his party boarded shortly after midnight on the 18 June. The heavy water was stowed with the diamond crates in a cabin next to the Master's, it only had one small porthole and the door was guarded by an armed sentry.

By now there were just over one hundred extra people on board. Cargo ships like the *Broompark* carry sufficient life jackets for the crew, of about forty, plus a few spares. There are also eight lifebuoys. A lifeboat is carried on each side, both capable of taking the full crew, the *Broompark* also had a smaller 'jollyboat' on the bridge structure. If the ship sank, and if it remained upright while it is doing so, about eighty people might get away in the boats.

Paulsen had issued all available life jackets before leaving Bordeaux, but there not even sufficient for the women and children, the rest had inner tubes taken from cars that had been loaded. The women were not told that there were no life jackets of any sort for the men. An entry in the Official Log records that a lifeboat drill was held and the boats were swung out.

Ocean Liberty **a very similar British designed ship built in the USA**
Courtesy ABS

The Merchant Navy

In 1939 Britain's merchant fleet was by far the largest in the World, with ships registered in all parts of what was then the Empire. Many ships were twenty or more years old and a considerable proportion had been laid up for years because of the slump. In that time seamen who had jobs hung onto them, while others trudged around the shipping offices looking for work. Master Mariners signed on as Able Seamen and Quartermasters; many left the industry altogether.

Until after the Great War the service had been known as the Mercantile Marine. In 1919 a standard uniform was authorized. Later it was renamed the British Merchant Navy, with the Sovereign becoming Master of the Merchant Navy and the Fishing Fleets. Then, and for years afterwards, it was referred to as The Merchant Service.

It never was a navy, but the title and the uniform were decided upon because of a problem that had occurred during the First World War. Captain Charles Fryatt, Master of the Railway Packet *Brussels*, had evaded and attempted to ram U-boats. When the Germans finally captured him they held that, as he was a civilian, he could not claim protection under the rules of The Hague Convention. He was tried in Belgium and shot that evening. In 1919 his body was exhumed and brought back to England; after a memorial service in St Paul's Cathedral he was reburied at Dovercourt, Harwich.

Both the quality of the ships and the conditions of employment varied widely. At best seamen were on given continuous employment, decent accommodation and food. At the worst, living conditions were disgusting and food was inadequate. Wages were stopped as soon as a ship sank, it was not until 1941 this practice was phased out. For the unfortunate men on the tramp ships conditions never really improved.

In addition to its peacetime role, which became essential for the Nation's survival, the merchant fleet would be needed to move war materials and troops, and to support evacuations and invasions. At the outbreak of the Second World War its total strength was only 157,000; about two thirds of the crews were from mainland Britain and the balance came from the Commonwealth and other countries.

A small number of women served on both British and allied vessels; several were awarded medals for bravery. One was Victoria Drummond, a God daughter of Queen Victoria, who served as an Engineer Officer. Miss Drummond was awarded the MBE and the Lloyd's War Medal for Bravery at Sea for single-handedly remaining at the controls of the cargo ship *Bonita* during an attack by a German bomber. She also volunteered for service at the Normandy landings.

In peacetime the merchant fleet brought sixty seven million tons of cargo into the UK annually. This included twenty two million tons of food, twenty eight and a half million tons of raw materials and nine and a half million tons of oil fuel. This met more than half of the country's meat requirements, 70% of its cheese and sugar, nearly 80% of fruits and about 90% of cereals and fats and all of the oil fuel. The ships brought in all the tobacco and tea, and much of the bread flour, that became so important once the war started. It is difficult to underestimate the importance of 'a cup of char, a sarnie and a fag' to the beleaguered people. One of the principal strategies of the Axis was to attack shipping bound for the UK, restricting British industry and with the intention of starving the nation into submission. In order to deal with the extreme shortages the Ministry of Food instituted a system of rationing.

Merchant ships are commanded by a Master. By 1939 a foreign-going ship carried a minimum of three Mates (also called Chief, Second and Third Officers); six or more Engineers; a Deck Department of eight under a Boatswain and a Carpenter; another eight ratings in the Engine Room, under a Donkeyman; a similar sized Catering Department and a single Radio Officer. There were usually between two and four Apprentices or Cadets. During the war most carried two more Radio Officers and about eight or more gunners from the Royal Artillery or the Royal Navy. On British ships these DEMS gunners were signed on as 'sailors' and were under command of the Master, one of the Mates being the Gunnery Officer.

Uniform was only worn by the officers on foreign-going ships. Petty officers and ratings usually wore dungaree trousers and shirts, with an old jacket in colder weather. They wore a wide variety of headgear from flat caps to hand-made nautical caps. Few on coastal cargo ships wore any kind of uniform. Earlier in the century some coastal masters had worn a bowler hat!

Ships that set out from the UK signed on a crew at the port of loading. With the exception of the Master, the First Mate and Chief Engineer and the Apprentices, the crew of a tramp would have been sourced in this way. In Merchant Navy slang they were known as a 'crowd' as in 'she had a Glasgow crowd.' The ships of the better companies were manned mostly, or even entirely, by 'company men.' Either way they signed Articles of Agreement which called for them to serve for a period of two years, or until they next returned to the UK. The 'Articles' set out their working conditions and the minimum amount of food they were to receive each month, known as 'the Board of Trade whack.' Different arrangements applied on coasters.

Ratings and petty officers were paid overtime for hours worked in excess of sixty four hours a week, though there were exceptions for days of arrival and sailing. Officers, engineers and apprentices were not usually paid overtime; this often resulted in the apprentices working considerably longer than the basic hours. Time spent on boat and fire drills or cleaning accommodation did not count towards the sixty four hours. A seaman had to provide his own clothing. Officers had to buy uniforms for tropical, temperate and Arctic service and the deck officers also bought their own sextants.

The British had begun developing 'Economy' ships like the *Broompark* in the early 1930s, though elements of the design came from much earlier. These were very basic ships that could carry up to 10,000 tons, including fuel, stores, crew etc. at a speed of about ten knots. The motor ships consumed ten tons of diesel oil per day, and for that reason they were sometimes known as 'ten, ten, tens.' The steamers burnt about twenty five tons of coal per day, with improved designs the steamers' fuel consumption was reduced below twenty tons per day.

Falmouth

When the *Broompark* arrived at 0630 on 21 June, there were ninety seven merchant ships in the port and a similar number elsewhere, mainly in Plymouth. Most had carried refugees from France.

Timbal woke from his sleep on the deck of the ship's hospital with his back sore and stiff. He realised that the ship was no longer moving he hurried to the porthole and found that it was daylight and in front of them were 'green meadows and friendly houses'. He roused his family. Some years later Kowarski described the Fal estuary as a beautiful harbour, though he and Timbal both noted that there were at least two sunken ships. Soon it was only 'those who had been in charge of our lives' who were sleeping, their job was done.

Nicolle records that they served a final meal to the passengers, who, it had been decided, would spend the coming night ashore in Falmouth. The afternoon was spent 'collecting all the blankets, enamel plate, forks, knives etc. which had been loaned to the passengers.' The car inner tubes were also collected.

Timbal says:

> I decided to try and clean up a little. To do this, I used a little Evian water, left over in one of the bottles, to wash my face and shave. My neck was as black as a coal miner's. My summer overcoat was stained with oil and coal. I put on another collar, my last clean one. I looked like a tramp in Sunday clothes.

He then started to fret about the diamonds, what would happen if the ship was bombed and sank in the harbour. At around ten o'clock several British Naval Officers boarded from a motor launch, they 'conferred with the Captain, Major Golding and the Earl of Berkshire.' A steam launch then brought a detachment of territorials aboard, their task being to guard the raft; the same launch took a number of British citizens ashore.

H M Customs and Excise were also concerned about the cargo; their unease was only heightened by one of the pair who seemed to be in charge. It was more than two hundred years since a pirate had last brought a cargo into Falmouth, claiming that he had 'saved' it from the French and even longer since one had said that the treasure he had was from the Spanish Netherlands.

Customs had no more reason to believe this than they would have believed one of the Earl's Tudor ancestors. They noted on the cover of file CUST 106/854 that he claimed that part of the lading was:

> A highly specialised and <u>secret</u> apparatus of which there is no duplicate anywhere in the world and which had been brought into the country <u>on ministerial directions</u> in the vital national interest *(their underlining)*.

Most of that was true, though the bit about ministerial direction was something of an exaggeration. It will be remembered that the British Embassy had a great deal of difficulty communicating with London and as far as the Admiralty knew the *Broompark* carried an 'unknown number of British citizens and machine tools.'

Lord Suffolk also said that the diamonds had been sent from the UK to Holland for cutting. This was probably only true of a portion of the consignment; though it was true that De Beers controlled the diamond trade through London.

An indecipherable note in the margin of the file gives the time of 1221 alongside a reference to 'Dr Gough Msc, M.B.E., F.R.S.' – someone was 'pulling rank.' The next paragraph is:

> On the grounds of urgency, these goods have been released without formality on landing. They were immediately removed by rail to their destinations, being accompanied by responsible members of the mission. An undertaking given by the Earl of Suffolk is annexed.

The Earl's scrawled note is there, including the words 'to wit', which he seemed fond of. There was a further note:

> Lord Suffolk was under the impression that the authority produced by him when the goods were imported was sufficient to dispense with all custom's formalities and also that they were of such special character that they were altogether outside the *(unclear word – definition?)* of merchandise.

In a postscript it is noted that a further 500 tons of valuable machinery is to be landed and retained in Falmouth until further instructions are received. It is interesting how the stated quantity changes. A later note says that 600 tons of machine tools are to be taken to the premises of the Motor Packing Co. Ltd. in Coventry.

Another note in the margin says that part of the consignment was sent to the Chief Engineer, Locomotive Department, GWR, (Great Western Railway) Swindon. Later Customs were told to 'let the matter of duty drop'.

Talking again about the stay in Falmouth, Timbal wrote:

> Towards noon, another motor launch came up to the ship. Two Naval officers of the Admiralty came on board. I was called by Major Golding and introduced to these officers. It appeared that I was to go with them and the Earl of Berkshire, in order to make arrangements with the Port authorities for the landing of the diamonds. The two officers were extremely polite. For the first time in my life I went down a rope ladder, down the side of a collier in order to get in a boat. It looks easy, but the ladder feels very unstable and the distance from the deck to sea seems terribly long.
>
> However, I got down safely into the launch and we headed towards the coast. I looked back; there, in the middle of the bay, lay our collier, doubly precious in my eyes. I hated to leave the ship, and the two wrecked boats I mentioned before did not reassure me. However, there was nothing else I could do. We landed at Falmouth and the Earl of Berkshire and I were led to the Customs authorities.

After some discussion it was decided that the raft and its contents should be put aboard the Custom/s launch, which would remain in shallow water.

The Earl sent a telegram to London:

OHMS PRIORITY = TRAINLOAD LEAVING SPECIAL TRAIN
FALMOUTH 2300 APPROX STOP WILL TELEPHONE
DEPARTMENT ON ARRIVAL = SUFFOLK AND BERKSHIRE.

Late in the afternoon the immigration people came aboard the ship.
Miss Nicolle spent the evening in the saloon helping with passports,
identity cards and immigration forms; when she emerged she found
that the rest of the mission had gone. By this time the ship was
alongside and an officer told her where to find Major Golding, when
she reached him she found that he had been looking for her. The town
was overwhelmed with landing evacuees. She was taken to a club
where sandwiches and a whisky were served. During the day there
had been a change of plan and they went to the railway station where
they boarded a train that Major Golding had arranged. Several reports
at this time comment on how polite and helpful the British officials
were, in marked contrast to those they had met in Belgium and
France.

On the train Golding and Nicolle managed to get a compartment to
themselves. The Timbal family were in another where they laid the
children down on the seats:

> Just then (it was almost midnight), we had our first taste of the
> kindness of a great people; Ladies of the British Red Cross (I had no
> idea who warned them, or who had even thought of warning them)
> went from one compartment to the other with hot tea and pieces of
> delicious freshly made cake. What a luxury after the stale bread we

47

had eaten for the last five days. We even received some warm milk for the children. My wife and the nurse could not restrain their tears. I also saw tears in the eyes of the Red Cross volunteer, a very kind and distinguished looking lady with white hair, who was helping us. We were far from the Germans. That cup of tea and piece of cake had comforted us morally as well as physically.

There are a number of accounts of this type: others were helped by the Women's Voluntary Service and the Women's Institute. The WI record, at the Dorset History Centre, shows that the people of the little port of Weymouth donated food, utensils and toiletries. They even set up a nappy changing service, where mothers could at least get a little rest. For the men there were free haircuts and shaves. This happened in ports all over the country.

The train set off and, as it steamed through the night, the exhausted passengers were able to grab some sleep.

During the day Lord Suffolk had telephoned the Ministry of Supply in London, he told the Director of Scientific Research, Dr H. J. Gough, of the arrangements that they had made and informed him that there were other scientists and officials who also wished to come to the UK. The list included:

Col.Dupui (Armour plate expert)
Col. Ott (in charge of Experimental Establishment at Bourges)
Capt. Bichelonne (M. Dautry's Chief of Staff)
Gen. Blanchard (Head of all the powder works in France)
Gen. Mitignon (equivalent to Director General of Design)

These people were last heard of in Bordeaux. Other names were added later. Suffolk had asked that a destroyer to be sent from Falmouth to embark these people, but the Naval Officer in Charge would not take responsibility without direct instructions from his Commander-in-Chief. Lord Suffolk was to find that his powers of persuasion had limits, as, except in a battle situation, naval officers could not act in this way. It was more than fortunate that Captain Paulsen, though unable to contact the ship's owners, had been quite prepared to embark the Mission, and all of its human and material acquisitions, in Bordeaux. Without his prompt decision there might not have been a story to tell.

The Minister authorised the Admiralty to send a signal to Bayonne regarding the transport of 'uranium ore and more technicians' to the United Kingdom. With this instruction the D.S.R. went to the Admiralty, where he found that the First Sea Lord was 'at a conference...and (DSR) waited till 7.0 p.m.' The Second Secretary at the Admiralty then got in touch with the Director of Operations and was told that, 'as there were a number of merchant ships in Bayonne, the Admiralty did not consider it necessary to send a special destroyer.'

The signal on this subject was not sent until almost a day later. Subsequently Major Golding was provided with a copy of a minute sheet, marked VERY SECRET P.S./Minister, which says that a signal was despatched on the 22 June. No times are given throughout the memo and there were no ships named, but other files show that the first signal was not sent until 1648 on 22 June. There followed a signal from H.M.S. *Berkeley*, also sent on the 22 June (at 2138), that he was not in touch with the B.N.L.O Bordeaux, or the British Ambassador. A 'second reply' was received from the B.N.L.O Bordeaux (at 2316) saying that the previous message was not received. This lack of timely action meant that further valuable equipment and key people were lost to the British. Then French Nationals were prevented from leaving by the terms of the Armistice which came into force on 25 June.

Lord Suffolk had listed the materials that they had on board:

Six hundred tons of machine tools.
3-million pounds worth of diamonds.
All the heavy water in France, from the Joliot-Curie laboratories.
The entire secret archives of the (French) Ministry of National Education together with the Under Secretary of State of that Ministry and one other officer.
Two pieces of apparatus of considerable scientific importance.
The secret documents belonging to himself and Golding from Paris
A new secret machine tool for the manufacture of 20mm Hispano-Suiza gun.
Another machine tool of similar nature
Some anti-aircraft guns
Twenty four French scientists and technicians of very high rank together with two pharmacologists and one ballistic expert.

After the DSR made the necessary arrangements, he had unsuccessfully tried to contact Suffolk again, leaving messages with the Chief of Police and the station master at Falmouth. He also wanted to tell the Earl that the Minister wished to see him as soon as possible. The Minister was Herbert Morrison and his deputy Harold Macmillan.

Dr. Gough did find out from the station masters at Falmouth and Paddington that the special train that Golding had arranged would not arrive at Paddington before 6 a.m. the following morning; so he arranged for his car to collect him at 5 a.m. to be there to meet it. He must have had a long wait as the train did not arrive until about nine.

Nineteen vessels sailed from the Gironde between 17 and 23 June, including two warships and several cargo liners, No reports explain the choice of the *Broompark*, who nevertheless did her job very well.

London

When the train pulled into Paddington station the waiting armed guards secured the platform. The carriage doors were locked and then the soldiers concentrated on the luggage van.

The passengers were anxious to get out, but the authorities wanted to arrange for the transport of the cargo first. In an effort to get out Timbal called out to the Earl of Suffolk who was passing. He was told to be patient and that the Earl would return as soon as he had 'conferred with the authorities of the station.'

After half an hour the Earl returned with the guard, who let the Timbal family and Van Campenhout alight, locking the carriage door behind them. They were introduced to the officer who was in charge of the military guard and allowed to pass the barrier.

Timbal saw that the crates of diamonds were still at the station, where an Army lorry was waiting. He was told that they would be loaded at about nine o'clock and taken to the Diamond Corporation, 8 Charterhouse Street, followed by another lorry with armed soldiers. He was asked to be there at ten.

There is a difference between the times that Miss Nicolle gives in her account and Timbal, who gives the train's arrival time as 8 a.m. I have used Nicolle's times as her account appears to have been written soon after the event, she says that the train arrived at nine. Timbal's was not completed until 1943, by which time he was in New York. Timbal accepted that he could do no more for the safety of his precious cargo, so he took his party to the Mayfair Hotel in a taxi.

When interviewed in the USA in 1969 Kowarski said that it was 'a typical British muddle'. Kowarski did admit that a lot of infiltration was going on; he noticed signs of fear, but agreed that it was justified. Timbal was also well aware of the British concern about the possibility of fifth columnists being within the group.

The conflict had affected those in the UK so little that they had, up till now, called it the Phoney War. But the newly appointed Winston Churchill warned them that he had little to offer but 'blood, sweat and tears.' On the 18 June in his 'Finest Hour' speech, he had warned them that the Battle of France was over and the Battle of Britain was about to begin. Small wonder that those who saw the steady streams of refugees and evacuees realised that the situation was every bit as bad as their new Prime Minister said.

When the party disembarked the secretaries escorted them across the station to the Great Western Hotel, where breakfast and rooms awaited them. Kowarski took his family to stay with his wife's relations. Halban moved to the Mayfair Hotel, where he must have been received rather like Timbal:

> I will always remember the surprise of the clerk at the reception desk when he saw us come in. Our clothes were worn, dirty and stained with oil. We looked exhausted. My wife had her mink coat rolled in a bath towel. This bath towel looked more like the baggage of a fifth class emigrant than that of people who wished to stay at a first class hotel in London.

I had the impression that we were about to be told that there were no rooms available in the hotel, when one of the assistant managers recognized me under my layer of coal dust.

"Mr. Timbal, where are you coming from?" he exclaimed I said "It's very simple … we have just come from the other side, and we are glad to be here, believe me!"

We were taken care of immediately. It was wonderful to have a nice clean bedroom; to be able to enjoy the quiet and comfort to which we are used to in our time. The servants busied themselves bringing towels … hot water was running in the baths. It was marvellous… We were afraid it was a dream!

After a quick bath and some bacon and eggs and a cup of tea, Timbal took a taxi to the Diamond Corporation. He arrived at same time as Major Golding's transport. The soldiers closed the two streets outside and all traffic was stopped. The activity quickly drew a crowd of onlookers, who gawped as the crates marked 'Banque Diamantaire Anversoise' were taken from the trucks.

Timbal said he thought of all those crates had gone through:

The roads of Belgium and the roads of France; the Compiègne Police Station; the Banque Transatlantique in Paris; again the French roads; then the Banque Transatlantique in Cognac; the French roads again; the British Consulate in Bordeaux; on board the Broompark; the train from Falmouth to London; the military trucks … and at last the Diamond Corporation.

His job was done and he could now think of his family's future. What is strange is that Timbal's account ends at this point; he makes no mention of the subsequent opening of the crates and packages.

After they had seen to the transfer of the heavy water and much else, Dr Gough the DSR had taken Lord Suffolk to see Harold Macmillan, who was deputising for the Minister Herbert Morrison. Much of the rest of the day was taken up with meetings.

On the 27 June Herbert Morrison gave the House a detailed description of the Ministry of Supply's work, ending:

> Now let me make a short reference to the scientific research department, which is under the direction of an exceedingly powerful committee of scientists, with Dr H. J. Gough, an eminent scientist, a Doctor of Science and Philosophy, a Fellow of the Royal Society and the Institute of Physics and a Member of the Institute of Mechanical Engineers at their head. They have an advisory council under the chairmanship of Lord Cadman, and they have done splendid work in scientific research for the Ministry, which obviously I cannot talk about. But I should like to assure the House that proper measures have been taken for the consideration and examination of all proposals of a scientific and inventive character, and no trouble or expense will be spared. That department is one of great privacy. I can assure the House that this fine body of scientists is doing splendid work.

According to Hansard the speech lasted for fifty six minutes. Immediately afterwards The Lord Privy Seal (Mr Attlee) called the

Speaker's attention 'to the fact that strangers are present.' The Speaker put the Question: 'That strangers be ordered to withdraw.' The Question was put, and agreed to and the Strangers withdrew accordingly. This is the rather quaint procedure for the House of Commons to go into Secret Session.

Papers at the National Archives in Kew, west of London, show that the Minister then made the following statement:

> As we are in secret session I am able to tell the House of a piece of work by two officers of the Ministry who were in Paris as Liaison Officers with the Ministry of Armament. These officers, with the co-operation of certain patriotic Frenchmen and the British Embassy, succeeded in obtaining a ship and arming it against attack from the air. This ship was loaded with, among other things, machine tools and large quantities of valuable and secret stores, some of them of almost incalculable scientific importance. There were also embarked on this ship, owing to the efforts that were made, a considerable party of key personnel consisting of eminent scientists and armament experts.

> In spite of an attempt to bomb it, this ship arrived safely in England and arrangements are being made for the personnel to continue their work in the service of the Allied cause and the stores have been safely disposed of.

> Although I cannot do so publicly I should like to pay tribute to the highly successful efforts of the representatives of the ministry and also to the members of the British Embassy and to the officers and

crew of the ship. A considerable service has been rendered to the Allied cause by the safe arrival of this shipload.

Presumably because the mission was top secret no awards are recorded. It is not made clear that the ship was a merchantman, and the two secretaries are not mentioned.

At first no one knew what to do with the heavy water. Until, on the 4 July, General Sir Maurice Taylor, a Senior Military Advisor (to the Ministry of Supply?) wrote to Lord Wigram at Windsor Castle telling him:

> We have rescued from France a small stock of what is probably the most valuable and rare material in the world and one which is most urgently needed, in very small quantities, for what we hope may prove to be without exaggeration the most important scientific contribution to our war effort.

He went on to ask 'if he could arrange safe storage 'in some small chamber in the depths below Windsor Castle'.

On 9 July Lord Suffolk collected twenty of the cans and delivered them to the Castle library, where the librarian O F Morshead took charge and arranged for the consignment to be stored in the same place as the Crown Jewels. No one could say that the British did not appreciate the value of the material that had been saved.

On 11 July Morshead wrote a note to Gough confirming arrangements for the release of the material and saying 'the King knows that it is here.' Morshead was much more than a librarian; his decorations were C.V.O. D.S.O. M.C. Croix de Guerre. By 1952 he was Sir Owen Frederick Morshead KC.V.O etc. and in 1958 K.C.B. Even in 1936 Lord Wigram's full style was Colonel the Right Honourable Clive, Baron Wigram G.C.B. G.C.V.O. C.S.I.

Twelve square tins of more concentrated material and eight round tins of less concentrated material were taken to Windsor. Three square tins and three round tins, with the same contents as the Windsor consignment, remained at Wormwood Scrubs prison – at that time the temporary headquarters of MI5.

Meanwhile on the 5 August the two diamond crates were removed from the strong room at the Diamond Corporation in the presence of a small group, which included M. Timbal and John Martyn Dimond, a Notary Public.

On the first crate the (wax?) seals, of the French Embassy in Brussels and Major Golding, were broken and the sixty eight packets were numbered and listed. Then the second smaller crate, which only had Major Golding's seal as it had previously been opened in Bordeaux where packages had been added, was opened; it contained thirty six packets. All were listed with the names of the depositors. The two crates were then repacked and resealed. The Notarised list was later used to show when the various packages were released, but it is difficult to read most of these notes.

On 8 August the crates were again opened, this time to remove eighteen packets that were destined for the USA. With the exception of one package, they were found to contain only rough or cut diamonds. Package No 82, which also contained jewellery, was resealed and left with the Diamond Corporation.

Operation Aerial

Operation Dynamo, the evacuation from Dunkirk, is well known to the British and the French, though for different reasons. Winston Churchill described it as 'a miracle of deliverance', while others called it 'the miracle of Dunkirk'. However there were a couple of myths of Dunkirk: one was that every last man of the British Expeditionary Force had been saved, in fact at least 130,000 of the troops remained at large in France.

The next rescue was attempted between 10 June and 13 June, from the ports of St Valery and Le Havre. During this Operation Cycle 14,557 British troops were saved and a similar number of French troops were ferried to Cherbourg, but 8,000 men of the British 51st Highland Division were cut off and ordered to surrender. Admiral W James said that the rescue 'fell far short of my early hopes'.

From 15 June the much larger, and ultimately more successful, Operation Aerial (or Ariel) was mounted. First Admiral James and, as the rescue moved westward, Admiral Dunbar-Naismith, took charge. By this time the numbers needing to be rescued included civilians from the Channel Islands and BEF reinforcements who had been landed at St Malo.

Once almost 140,000 BEF troops were saved from Brittany it became obvious that the rescue would have to be extended to ports in western and southern France. Many Polish and Czech troops, and civilians, still needed to be brought back to the UK, as did many British civilians.

St Nazaire became the scene of Britain's worst maritime disaster when the liner *Lancastria* was bombed and sank, about 3,000 perished. Churchill prevented the news of the disaster reaching the British public, and, with it, the news of the otherwise successful Operation Aerial.

Because of their losses at Dunkirk the Royal Navy was desperately short of ships. They continued to organise the rescue, but it fell to the merchant ships to carry the troops and civilians to safety. Many of these ships were sent from the UK, but others were requisitioned at the evacuation ports.

The evacuation of Bordeaux continued for several days after the *Broompark* had sailed.

At 1312 on 20 June the *Berkeley* was ordered by the Admiralty to get in touch with Feller & Co., 1, Espirit de Lois, Bordeaux, and arrange shipment of vital goods ex. Goth Co., Switzerland. These included Oerlikon guns, spares and probably drawings. One file states that 'valuable stores' had been shipped on *Swift* (General Steam Navigation Co. had a ship of this name) on 17 June.

On 22 June the B.N.L.O Bordeaux was informed by the Admiralty that s.s. *Formedine* (*Fort Medine*?), with a valuable cargo of copper and machine tools, should be sailed without delay. The French ship *Le Trait* was included in the series of messages, but she was diverted to North Africa, with the goods ex Goth Co. The French Admiralty had already moved a large quantity of Belgian gold to a 'safe destination' outside France. Admiral Darlan was not willing to tell the British or the Belgians where (see the chapter: Other *Rescues*). *Le Trait* remained under the French flag throughout the war, while the *Fort Medine* was seized by the British on arrival in Falmouth. Also during the night of 22 June the French ship *Louis L D*, with a general cargo, 'deserted' convoy HX50, she had been destined for Belfast, and this act of barratry deprived the British of 7,000 tons of valuable cargo.

At 1730 the *Imogen* reported numbers evacuated as: *Witch* 340, *Viscount* 500 and herself with 466, including three British and fourteen Belgian soldiers. At 2130 the Master of the French ship *Gravelinnes* asked for food for the 500 people on board. At 2258 the following were sent to the Gironde with orders to report to any British warship on arrival: the *Delius, Glenaffric, Clan Ferguson, Blairnevis, Cyclops, Beckenham, Clan Ross, Balfe, Kyno, Kuffra, Kelso, Maplewood, Calumet* and *Baron Nairn*. The signal said that the *Royal Scotsman* should have already arrived there. Another signal added that the *Ormonde*, with a capacity of 5,000, was also due at the Gironde; and the *Batory* with a capacity of 3,000 had been ordered to Bayonne. These, and other ships, had their destination ports changed, sometimes several times.

The *Ettrick* reported that she was off the entrance to Bayonne and had been informed by the signal station that she was too large to enter. She requested further instructions and was told to stay under way in the vicinity and await orders.

At 1930 the *Berkley* informed *Vanquisher* that she was with the *Clan Ferguson* and *Royal Scotsman* (also *Blairnevis*) with 4,000 Polish troops, leaving Le Verdon at 2115 for Liverpool and that the *Delius* would follow on 23 June with another 2,000. The embarkation of 6,000 Poles was completed and *Delius* sailed at 0915, unescorted. By this time *Beagle* was short of fuel.

The French refused to permit further embarkation 'without British assistance.' Polish officers were remaining to divert the Poles to Bayonne; it was suggested that *Beckenham* 'be diverted thither.' When they were approaching the River Gironde HMCS *Fraser* was cut in half when she was rammed by the Cruiser *Calcutta*, the fore part sank. HMCS *Restigouche* was ordered to sink the after part, after recovering survivors.

On the cargo ship *Calumet* AB Tommy Thomson wrote in his diary:

> We were sent post-haste to Bordeaux to try to rescue some troops retreating from the Germans. But when we got within sight of the land, a lighthouse at the mouth of the Gironde called us up by Morse lamp, to say that the Germans were in the town, and it was too late. So the ship was put about for England, and we arrived back in Falmouth on 25 June.

It was decided that the small port of St Jean de Luz, near Bayonne, offered better loading prospects, so it was from there that the Senior Naval Officer reported that 'no less than 9,000 Poles' sailed in the *Sobeiski* & *Batory* on 21 June. These ships were not escorted, but arrived safely at Plymouth on 24 June. It was also reported that British refugees embarking in the *Ettrick* would require close examination as there were some 'doubtful cases among them.' Poles continued to arrive and it was intended that the next embarkation would be on the *Arandora Star*. The SNO enquired when the *Arandora Star* might be expected and stated that *Fraser* had been 'withdrawn'. At 1000 on 23 June he signalled that the *Ettrick* had been loaded with 1,000 refugees and another 3,000 had arrived. At noon he added "am now filling *Ettrick* to capacity by embarking 300 Poles and asked 'when may we expect another ship?' When *Ettrick* sailed she was said to be 'full to capacity' with 2,000 troops.

At 1523 C in C WA informed Admiralty that it was understood that 49,000 troops still required evacuation so *Belgravian, Baron Nairn, Baron Kinnard, Kerma* were sent to Bayonne. At 2100 on 23 June all embarkation ceased at St Jean de Luz, owing to the heavy swell. All on the *Ettrick* watched. In the words of the British nurse Miss R Andrews from the American Hospital of Paris, who had boarded from a sardine boat:

> On Monday afternoon the huge s.s. *Arandora Star* came steaming in and to the astonishment of everybody slowly manoeuvred into the tiny harbour of St Jean de Luz. She was much bigger than our *Ettrick* and sat in the harbour towering above the fishing village. By 6 p.m she had loaded up and gingerly extricated herself from the harbour.

The *Arandora Star* had mostly embarked troops of the Polish Army and Air Force; a signal added that Polish forces would require close scrutiny. At 1430 2,600 Poles remained at St Jean de Luz. The cargo ship *Clan Ross* was attacked by aircraft at 1344 when she was 30 miles NNW of St Jean de Luz. *Clan Ross*, and the empty *Cyclops, Kerma, Glenaffric, Belgravian* and *Beckenham*, were escorted back to the UK by the *Mackay* and *Viva II*.

65

On 23 June the Polish drifters *Delfin II, Korab I* and *Korab II* had arrived at Barry Dock with Polish soldiers from La Rochelle. That evening SNO sent a signal pointing out that C in C's signal of 2356/22, refusing permission to embark wives and families, was 'causing difficulties and heart rending scenes.' He asked if he could promise embarkation after priority commitments had been fulfilled, saying that it was impossible to be sure of the identity of any of those who wished to board. At 0731 on 25 June the C in C signalled that the wives and families of Polish soldiers could be embarked 'if accommodation available' and approximately 2,000 womenfolk embarked in the *Batory* and *Sobieski*. These were presumably included in the 9,000 total that these Polish liners had on board. Because of the earlier crew trouble, Captain Pacewicz was relieved on arrival at Plymouth and Captain Deyczakowski took command; at the same time the armed guard disembarked.

The small cargo ship *Kelso* replaced the *Arandora Star* at the loading berth and only when enemy aircraft were sighted, and with the armistice in force, did she and the *Baron Kinnard* sail for Liverpool, with a total of 2,000 troops. They reached their destination in four days. The *Baron Nairn* also sailed for Falmouth for the same reason, with 1,200 Polish troops and British refugees aboard. Food must have been a problem, even in peacetime the Baron ship's owners were known throughout the service as 'Hungry Hogarth's.'

Just over a week later the *Arandora Star* was torpedoed, of the 1,673 on board, 470 Italian and 243 German POWs died, plus thirty seven guards. Captain Moulton, twelve officers and forty two crew members also lost their lives.

As we have seen the Operation Aerial evacuation continued until the Armistice came into force on 25 June and that morning the last three British cargo ships sailed from St Jean de Luz with a total of 3,200 evacuees, including many Polish troops. The day before the trooper *Ettrick* had sailed from there with 1,100, including King Zog of Albania and his entourage. Early in the morning of the 24th HMS *Galatea* had sailed for home:

> carrying, in addition to Embassy Staff, 1 Flight Lt. R.A.F., 1 Lt, ex French Air Force, 1 Lt. R.N.V.R. *(Fleming)*, 1 Air Ministry Official, 5 R.A.F. ranks, 4 army ranks. Wounded:- 1 Army Officer, 3 ranks, 1 R.A.F. rank, 14 bags valuables for Polish Finance Minister.

At 1721 on 25 June the C in C informed the Admiralty that it was intended to release merchant ships reserved for Aerial as no further requirement could be foreseen: the Armistice had come into force.

On 28 June the trawlers *St Malante* and *Bervie Braes*, arrived at Plymouth at 0724 and the *Baron Nairn* arrived at 0735 with refugees from St Jean de Luz and anchored in Cawsand Bay. A small French fishing boat with twelve male refugees also arrived at Cawsand at 0750, and one minute later the *Glenaffric* passed the signal station at Plymouth.

Operation Aerial was over, though refugees continued to arrive. At 0825 the French Fishing vessel *Dom Michel Nobletz* arrived from Ushant with one British and seven French refugees, thirty three sailors and seven soldiers. She was also without food and water.

In all over 186,000 British, Polish and Czech troops, plus a few Belgians were saved during Operation Aerial; there are no reliable figures for the number of civilians saved at the same time.

Some of the 3,500 evacuees on the *Alderpool*, this ship ran out of food and water long before arriving in Plymouth. Courtesy: Halina Macdonald and the Polish Institute and Sikorski Museum, London.

The Fifth Column

The term Fifth Columnist may not be as familiar as it was to the readers in the 1940s, the newspapers were full of tales of uprisings that preceded the Germans. It was first used by the Nationalist General Emilio Mola during the Spanish Civil War. When interviewed in 1936 he said that a fifth column inside Madrid would rise up in support of his four columns, when they neared the city.

Some idea of the effect of these people can be judged by extracts from the file Military and Naval Operations in Holland in May 1940:

> The action of the fifth column, especially active in The Hague, must be noted here. It consisted mainly of German residents in Holland and naturalised Germans. The Dutch Nazis formed only a very small minority. Like the parachutists, the fifth column made ample use of disguises and caused considerable confusion by sniping at the Dutch police and the civilian population. Among the disguises employed were those of postmen, policemen, tram conductors and even women and priests. False rumours were also used as effective weapons by these organised gangsters. Thus they spread rumours about orders for evacuation, alleged to be given by the authorities, warnings against non-existent poisoned cigarettes and chocolates etc. ….

> On this day *(11 May)* they were strongly supported by the fifth column, operating in The Hague with great violence, but failing to check the continuous hunting out of paratroopers. … The threat of the fifth column to the centre of the country, however, remained.

Further on there is a reference to 'German artillery hiding amongst the cargo of a Swedish ship, which had been in Rotterdam for some time.'

In the Operation Aerial journal (Appendix Five) there are several notes like: 'British refugees embarking in *Ettrick* will require close examination as doubtful cases among them.' Suspects were also attempting to board with Polish and Czech troops and even, in one case, with a group of British and Irish seminarians.

There were also difficulties with a number of ships from Europe. In some instances the crews were suspected of having Nazi sympathies and in others the passengers refused to endure the discomfort of having to make the trip with additional refugees.

Because of the shortage of shipping in Bordeaux seven Dutch ships were requisitioned to supplement the British and Polish ships that were already employed.

According to John de S Winser, the *Nigerstroom*, 'having agreed to take 500-600 British evacuees, ejected them after boarding, to preserve the comfort of the Dutch passengers already on board.' However this ship is recorded as carrying six hundred British passengers from Le Verdon to Falmouth. It would seem that an armed guard from HMS *Arethusa* caused this change of mind. Winser also says that the Dutch *Berinice* and *Orpheus* refused to embark any refugees. This did not stop the *Orpheus* seeking British convoy protection from December 1940.

It should be said that two British ships were boarded by armed guards during the Dunkirk evacuation. The crew grouses being that they were exhausted and, while on the homeward trips the troops had some Bren guns, on the outward trips the ships were unarmed. In the case of one ship a doctor confirmed that the whole crew were exhausted and unfit to continue.

Members of the mission, and others attempting to save people and valuables, would have been in a most difficult situation. The men were all armed and were attempting to deprive the Germans of what they would have regarded as the spoils of war. Only Major Golding, and possibly M. Timbal as a reserve officer, would have been entitled to prisoner of war status. The others were civilians and might well have been judged to be spies or *francs-tireurs*.

The Holy Trinity

The Earl retrained as a bomb disposal officer, he then formed a three person bomb disposal team that he called The Holy Trinity, or The Trinity; sources disagree, as they disagree about who first came up with the name. The Trinity were the Earl, Eileen Beryl Morden and his driver, Fred Hards. They made a name for their skill in detecting and successfully defusing thirty four bombs.

Morden stood by the Earl's side taking notes that he dictated while at work; the idea being that, in the event of failure, there would be a record that would show what went wrong. Only at the last moments would Morden seek shelter. Hards was a handyman, able to arrive at practical solutions for all kinds of problems; the Earl was also a very practical individual, but no man can do it all.

The Wikipedia article, Charles Howard, 20th Earl of Suffolk, by various contributors says:

> An official report underlined the strain of his work: "On many occasions Lord Suffolk cleared everyone away from the danger area and proceeded to operate alone. Deliberately he exposed himself daily to danger." Jack was a fatalist saying that "If my name is on a bomb, that's it." Sadly, the thirty-fifth claimed its forfeit when all three were killed on Erith Marshes in Kent on 12 May 1941.
>
> The bomb, a 250 kg (500 lb.) weapon, was at one of the so-called 'bomb cemeteries', on open ground on the marshes. Bombs were

transferred here after being temporarily made safe for transport, and then destroyed using controlled explosions. The bomb had been dropped some six months earlier in the previous autumn and after removal and transfer to the marshes had been at Erith for so long it had been known to the Sappers as 'Old Faithfull'.

Containing two separate fuses, a Type (17) and a Type (50), these two types were in short supply to the Bomb Disposal Sections, intact fuses being required for instructional purposes and it was for the purpose of recovering the fuses that the Earl was dealing with bomb. The Type (17) was a delayed-action fuse containing a clockwork mechanism, while the Type (50) was an anti-handling device containing a motion sensor. Both fuses had been temporarily made-safe so that the bomb could be transferred from the impact site to an open area; however the fuses remained inside the bomb. In addition the Germans had also implemented on some bombs a *Zus 40* booby-trap, that detonated the bomb when an attempt was made at withdrawing the Type (17). The *Zus 40* was positioned below the other fuse, and so was not visible until the obvious fuse was partially withdrawn from its pocket.

At lunchtime of the 12th May the Earl had telephoned his office to say that the Type (17) was ticking and that he had sent for a Mk II KIM clock-stopper. By 14:45 this was in place along with a stethoscope, and preparations were being made to sterilise the bomb with steam. As two Sappers were going to fetch water for the steamer, the bomb exploded. The explosion killed the Earl, Hards, Morden - who died in the ambulance - and eleven *(?)* other people who had been nearby, including five Sappers who had been working alongside the Earl on the bomb. It was later surmised that a *Zus 40* may have been triggered as the Earl was removing it.

Sir Winston Churchill wrote about the tragedy in the second volume of his book *The Second World War*. The Earl also has a role in Michael Ondaatje's novel, *The English Patient*.

The Earl was awarded the George Cross. In the same Supplement to The London Gazette (35220 15 July 1941) there were Commendations for 'brave conduct in Civil Defence' for 'Frederick William Hards (deceased), Van Driver, and Miss Eileen Beryl Morden (deceased), Shorthand -Typist - both from the Experimental Unit, Ministry of Supply.'

Miss Morden is buried in a council grave with three others. When the grave was traced by Chris Ranstead, her name was misspelt as Norden - Mr Ranstead had this corrected, but there is no room for a mention of the Commendation. It may have been that only the George Cross and a Commendation can be awarded to civilians posthumously, this would account for what appears to be a rather niggardly treatment of this brave woman, and the equally brave Mr Hards.

Geoffrey Gillon has posted a photograph of Miss Morden's grave, and the book of commemoration with an entry about Mr Hards, on the UK site Find a Grave. On the same site Kevin Brazier has posted several photographs of the Earl's grave, the foot stone has a carving of his George Cross.

A stained glass window designed by Gerald Smith of St. John's Wood was dedicated by Frederick Cockin the Bishop of Bristol at a special service on the afternoon of Monday 15, September 1947 at the church of St. John the Baptist, Charlton; the family church.

At the bottom of the panel is the Suffolk family coat of arms. In the right hand light is a picture of ss *Broompark*, the vessel in which the Earl made his escape from Bordeaux in France. The picture shows the moment a German plane appeared above the ship, but flew off without attacking. In the left hand light is a picture of the sailing vessel *Mount Stewart*, on which the Earl was an apprentice.

Two scenes are depicted in detail. One shows work taking place in a laboratory, the other the dangerous business of bomb disposal. Above the bomb disposal squad is the inscription in memory of the Earl and those who died with him. Finally, above the scene in the laboratory is displayed a poem by John Masefield, Poet Laureate (himself a former sailing ship apprentice), written by him upon hearing the news of Jack Howard's death:

> He loved the bright ship with the lifting wing;
> He felt the anguish in the hunted thing;
> He dared the dangers which beset the guides;
> Who lead men to the knowledge nature hides;
> Probing and playing with the lightning thus;
> He and his faithful friends met death for us;
> The beauty of a splendid man abides.

Secondary accounts have made the story somewhat Suffolk centric, probably because Lord Suffolk was such a colourful character; but as Colonel Golding said in a letter to *The Sunday Times on* 27 March 1960:

> I am sure Lord Suffolk, if he were alive today, would wish me to say that the task, though interesting and unusual, was not 'fantastic' and was no more dangerous than any routine evacuation under the conditions. It would also seem that he would have wished the important part played by his three colleagues to be recognised.

Writers

The British expatriates living around Cape Ferrat expected 'a cruiser' to evacuate them in the style that they felt was their due; in the event they had to embark on two 'overcrowded filthy ships' that had recently discharged their coal cargoes in Toulon. One of these ships had 'only two lavatories.' Several vessels picked up at more than one port and then sailed independently from France, arriving at Gibraltar between 26 and 30 June. One woman, who remained behind, said that her friends had written that they had to suffer these conditions all the way to Liverpool.

The two tramp ships were the *Ashcrest* and the *Saltersgate*. They had discharged their coal cargoes in Toulon and, after two days when their crews did their best to clean the ships, boarded a total of 1,300 refugees, mostly civilians. From Cannes they sailed first to Marseilles, where the refugees were forbidden to land. The Masters were instructed to join a French convoy bound for Oran; other evacuees, including some Poles, went to Oran in French ships.

The author W. Somerset Maugham was on the *Saltersgate*. He wrote about the voyage in these tramp steamers in *Strictly Personal* – which was first published by William Heinemann in 1941. Some of his recollections, written soon after the event are comic, while others are tragic. He says 'One lady, when she came aboard, told an officer that of course she wanted to go first class, and another called the steward (there was only one) and asked him to show her where the games deck was. 'It's all over the ship, madam,' he replied'. Somerset

Maugham also describes the hardships of the voyage on which several people died and four 'went out of their minds.'

Twenty two merchant ships were employed in the evacuation from the south of France. Two ships of the Royal Navy were there to organise the operation. It is not clear whether the numbers of those rescued are included in the Operation Aerial figures.

Whether by accident or design the British author P G Woodhouse was still in his villa at Le Touquet when the Germans arrived. He spent the next four years in various parts of Europe. At first he was detained as an Enemy Alien, then, a few months before his sixtieth birthday, he was released and remained in Paris until it was liberated.

The RNVR Lieutenant, who flew from London to Châteaudun airfield with Paul Timbal and travelled to Tours with him, reappears with radio equipment for the Embassy at Bordeaux. He seems to have made an impression on several ladies. When writing about her British team's arrival in Bordeaux Nurse R Andrew, of the American Hospital in Paris, says:

> Here we met an adorable young man in Naval Uniform, apparently the British Consul had beat it back to England and left him in sole command.

From there he went to Le Verdon, where he seems to have been one of the many who claim that they spent time persuading merchant shipmasters to take refugees, which they were already doing. He was probably invited to go forth.

On 21 June there were also forty 'English' nurses waiting to embark in Bordeaux. This may have been the Hadfield/Spears Volunteer Ambulance unit, of about twenty five, plus MTC drivers. According to a Wikipedia article the group were directed to Arcachon, further down the coast, by the British Military Attaché.

'At a villa outside the town, they met the British naval lieutenant Ian Fleming.' This is the first time that the lieutenant is named. Fleming was, at that time, a Lieutenant RNVR and personal assistant to Rear Admiral John Godfrey, the Director of Naval Intelligence. He was promoted to Lieutenant Commander in September 1940.

Fleming had flown 'to Paris' on 13 June. He is recorded as having got funds from the safe in the Rolls Royce office in the city; for this to have happened Fleming must have had the swiftest of transport, for the city fell on the next day. All the other parties found even making progress among the exodus extremely difficult. A picture emerges of a young man who could already 'spin a good yarn.'

In Arcachon Fleming arranged for the members of the nursing unit to be taken aboard HMS *Galatea,* which carried them south to St Jean de Luz, near the Spanish border. Here they transferred to the trooper *Ettrick.* The article then says that the ship 'already had on board a large number of British subjects (mainly well-to-do ladies and their staff) evacuated from their villas in France.' Fleming also travelled on the *Galatea*; Nurse Andrew says:

We were to meet him again in Bayonne and St Jean de Luz still in command of this army of refugees, still in perfect command – I hope he got a medal for it. And he was certainly whom biographer John Pearson had him (?) in Bordeaux organising the evacuation of the entire British refugee population during one afternoon there. He told us the Consulate had evacuated itself out of Bordeaux on a small boat en route for England.

In St Jean de Luz Fleming set about arranging for King Zog of Albania, and his entourage, to board the *Ettrick*. Even at this time of crisis Heads of State were normally carried by warships, so the deposed King Zog must have been regarded as only a minor person.

The British government would only give Zog temporary refuge on condition that he would move on to the USA; but he and his party remained in the UK, at first asking for help to recover their 119 items of luggage from Spain. Though Nurse Andrew records:

> On Monday morning King Zog of Albania arrived with his sisters, his wife, his young baby, his retinue, his servants, his treasure (his country's state treasure as we later learnt later in huge long metal coffins one of which nearly fell into the water) came aboard.

It would seem that they never went the America; so it is surprising that Fleming ever got promoted to Lieutenant Commander, having caused the government such inconvenience.

Could the decisive, pistol carrying, 'Wild Jack' Howard, Ardale Golding and Paul Timbal be the characters who were the original inspiration for Ian Fleming's spy James Bond? That would make the secretaries the first Bond girls, though one doubts that they would have relished the title.

Fleming once said that Bond 'was a compound of all the secret agents and commando types I met during the war.' More recently some writers have said that Bond was meant to be a Commander RNR, though how they surmise this is not known, this would make him a merchant service officer. It is noticeable that Fleming does not make him an RNVR officer.

As they say at sea:

> The Royal Navy are gentlemen, trying to be sailors;
> The Royal Naval Reserve are sailors, trying to be gentlemen;
> The Royal Naval Volunteer Reserve are neither, trying to be both.

Fleming returned to Plymouth on the *Galatea,* with him were the Embassy staff from Bordeaux. He would not have known that his hero, Somerset Maugham, was at sea at the same time. The older man and his fellow passengers endured real hardship, spending almost three weeks sleeping first in the hold with the coal dust, then, after Gibraltar, in the forecastle among the ropes and stores. When they arrived in Liverpool they had all lost a great deal of weight and were still in the clothes that they had worn when they boarded the *Saltersgate.* The *Saltersgate* was so decrepit that she was scuttled in 1944, to form part of the Gooseberry breakwater for the Mulberry harbour at Normandy.

When writing his books Fleming did draw on his past experiences; particularly in *Moonraker,* where a Ministry of Supply officer is shot dead and Bond to takes over his identity. The beautiful Gala Brand, an undercover Special Branch officer, has bluffed her way in to be the Personal Assistant to the villain, Sir Hugo Drax. Gala tells Bond that she is named after the warship HMS *Galatea*, which her father commanded at the time of her birth. Another of his characters is Felix Leiter, the surname was Lady Suffolk's maiden name. The Real Bond family owned lands in the Isle of Purbeck, near Fleming's school; they were not titled, but they gave their name to Bond Street in London.

The *Saltersgate*, with refugees. Courtesy John Schaffa

Afterwards

On 22 June *Broompark* was instructed to sail for Swansea. In fact she sailed for British Columbia on 25 June, back under MOWT control. In Canada she loaded lumber (sawn timber) and other cargo.

On the return voyage in convoy HX72 she was torpedoed and almost thrown on her beam ends. Most of the crew were saved by a corvette, though one fireman drowned. Captain Paulsen and seven of his deck and engineer officers remained on board and began the delicate business of righting the ship using water ballast. Then the balance of the crew re-boarded and the *Broompark* resumed her homeward voyage.

Though she was bombed and machine gunned while approaching the UK, Paulsen brought his ship safely home. For this he was made an Officer of the Order of the British Empire (OBE) and awarded Lloyd's Medal for Gallantry at Sea. Shortly after that he joined the Denholm's Superintendent's Department, where he remained for the rest of the war.

On Friday 4 December 1942 he wrote to his family from Port Alberni on Vancouver Island in British Columbia. He was then standing by a new ship being built for the Ministry of War Transport and to be managed by the Denholm Line.

Without this quiet unassuming man the mission might well have not succeeded. It was he who was prepared to take the responsibility of embarking the members of the Mission, and others: loading their possessions, in the knowledge that this might make his ship a particular target. He decided to go ahead, even though he could not get in touch with the ship's owners, in the knowledge that failure would have cost him his job, or even his life, and the lives of his crew and the passengers – quite a man!

M. Timbal and M. Ansiaux, Baron Ansiaux as he became, continued to be important figures in the Belgian banking industry after the war. Despite Lord Suffolk's best efforts, Captaine Bichelonne and the others who had greatly helped the mission were refused permission to leave France because of the Armistice. Bichelonne died in hospital in Germany in 1944 in mysterious circumstances. Had he survived he would have been tried by the French as a collaborator; he would have been accused of supplying French slave labour to the Germans.

There is no record of the eight tons of uranium ore and eighty tons of tolite (as spelt in signal from First Sea Lord's private office - possibly pectolite, a mineral) being saved from France.

Major Golding became a Colonel and retired in 1956, he died in Nantucket in 1992. No Marguerite Nicolles were born in the Channel Islands in the early 1900s, but a seven year old with that name was living in Chelsea, London, in 1911. In 1960, when Colonel Golding wrote her a reference, she was living in Fontainebleau. Ian Golding has found that a Marguerite Nicolle died on 17 July 1998 in the UK.

The scientists went on to have distinguished careers and played themselves in a post war film about the epic, a Google search produces a great deal about their careers.

In 1940 James Chadwick forwarded a file on the work of Halban and Kowarski to the Royal Society. He asked that the papers be held, as he felt that they were not appropriate for publication during the war. In 2007 the Society rediscovered the documents during an audit. When opened it was found that they described how to control the chain reaction, listed the components of a nuclear reactor, and described how to produce plutonium from uranium and therefore an atomic bomb.

At the opening Professor Brian Cox said 'I can see why these papers were locked away during the war, they contain details that could be used to build a nuclear reactor.' First Halban, and then Kowarski, went to Canada to co-operate with the Americans on what became the Manhattan project, the development of the atomic bomb. After the war Kowarski became a Deputy Director of CERN.

Wikipedia has information on the use of the heavy water and the development of nuclear reactors and the atomic bomb. For further reading a Wikipedia search for the two scientists, the MAUD Committee and Tube Alloys Ltd will be a start.

In 'A Friend's Tribute' in The Times of 21 May 1941, H.J.G. wrote an appreciation of Lord Suffolk. It is probably safe to assume that this piece was by Dr H J Gough; in it he writes about the Earl's complex and interesting character:

> By the recent death due to enemy action, of Charles Henry George Howard, twentieth Earl of Suffolk and thirteenth Earl of Berkshire this country has lost the services of a very gallant gentleman,

possessing an unusually wide and varied knowledge of men, affairs, and things, allied with a fearless and forceful personality tempered with great charm of manner and infinite courtesy and tact. A deep, almost fierce, devotion to duty; with work to be done almost all obstacles and restrictions, human or material, which threatened the allotted objective, were firmly overcome or circumvented, yet in such a manner that no sense of grievance remained except in the petty minded.

He goes on to describe an impromptu supper party, which went on into the early hours, where the Earl entertained his companions in English and in fluent French, in Cockney 'rhyming slang' and Chicago gangster argot. At some point in the party he produced his pistols 'Oscar' and 'Genevieve;' others have written about his fondness for his brace of pistols.

On the 3 July 1940 the Charlton Estate Office dispatched a crate (to London?). It contained a repeating shot gun, a repeating rifle and a pistol, together with ammunition for these guns. Also included were '150 rounds of .32 Automatic Pistol Cartridges – Reserved for the use of Lord Suffolk'; presumably for his pair of pistols. They would have been with him when he died. The rifle and the other pistol were destroyed when the team's Experimental Van burned out. The shot gun had been loaned to the Westminster Home Guard.

Bordeaux became the base of the Italian Submarine Service. The British only returned once before 1945, when a group from the Special Boat Service made the trip up the Gironde to scuttle shipping in Bordeaux. The film 'The Cockleshell Heroes' was made about this raid.

Other Rescues

By early May 1940 it became obvious that the Low Countries, though they had declared themselves to be neutral, were under threat.

On 11 May the Royal Navy's cruiser HMS *Arethusa* and the destroyer HMS *Boreas* escorted the Dutch ship *Iris* from Ijmuiden. On the same day HMS *Keith* escorted the steamer *Titus*, also from Ijmuiden. Both vessels carried Dutch government gold. They reached the Thames on the following morning. As they were not expected they were diverted to Folkestone, after being inspected by the British Naval Control Service.

On 13 May HMS *Vimy* escorted another bullion carrier the *Perseus*, again from Ijmuiden, with more of the Dutch gold. Also on that day another British destroyer, HMS *Walpole* brought industrial diamonds out of Holland.

The final attempt to save the Central Bank gold turned to disaster. Officials at the *Nederlandsche Bank*, The Dutch Central Bank, refused to release the bullion until they had a 'signature'. For this Cdr. J A Corrie Hill RN and two naval ratings had to travel to Rotterdam from the Hook; where Corrie Hill was in charge of XD B, the British contribution to the demolition work there. Once Corrie Hill had signed for the gold it was loaded onto the pilot vessel *BV.19A* at the Boompjes, the quay near the Bank.

On the next day, while sailing down the Nieuwe Waterweg to the sea, the pilot boat was destroyed by a magnetic mine. The ship sank with the gold. Sixteen of the twenty two men on board were killed and were buried at Vlaardingen cemetery, with full military honours. Much of the gold was salvaged for the Germans and more was recovered after the war.

On 14 May, only hours before the Netherlands fell, Gertruda Wijsmuller-Meyer brought eighty Jewish children to the docks in Ijmuiden. There she put them on the Dutch merchant ship *Bodegraven*. The ship was machine gunned during the voyage, but it reached Liverpool safely. Thus *Bodegraven* was the last of the *kindertransports*, a name more commonly given to the trains that carried these children to safety from Germany.

The Belgian government's pre-war gold reserves were about six hundred tons. One third was moved to North America and the Belgian Naval Trawler *A4* carried almost another third to Britain, sailing on 19 May, just before the Germans invaded. The gold and bank notes that she carried were valued at B.Fr. 2.500.000.000. The gold was finally landed at the British naval port of Plymouth on 26 May, two days before the Belgian surrender; from there it was taken to the Bank of England.

As the threat of invasion increased a further 198 tons of gold, packed in 4,944 chests, were taken from Ostend to Bordeaux. This consignment was stored in the vaults of the *Banque de France* there and at Libourne. This only left about forty tons in Belgium.

With the invasion of France underway the National Bank of Belgium understood that the bullion would be shipped overseas, to the United

States. Instead it was taken from Lorient to Dakar in French West Africa on 18 June. From there it was moved to Kayès, in the Sahara, about five hundred kilometres from Dakar.

When Hubert Ansiaux, by then representing the Bank in London, found this out he issued the French with a notice of default. Ansiaux had been on *A4*, but he must have returned to France as the Ansiauxs were passengers on the *Broompark*, as were Mme Ansiaux's parents.

Still worse was to come; as part of the Armistice settlement the French government had agreed to make the gold available to the Germans. Under pressure from the Vichy government the *Banque de France* reluctantly allowed the gold to be transferred.

By May 1942 the gold was moved, this time to Marseilles via Algiers and from there to the vaults of the *Reichsbank*. Göring ordered that it be seized and melted down in the Prussian *Staatsmünze*. It was hallmarked with the dates 1936 and 1937 so that it would appear to be German gold. After the war the *Banque de France* repaid the Belgium National Bank in full.

In April 1945 American troops discovered a massive store of treasures in a salt mine near the Thüringian town of Merkers. There were works of art, valuable objects looted by the SS, plus a stock of *Reichsbank* gold, probably including part of the gold belonging to the National Bank. The National Bank submitted a claim for compensation on behalf of the French central bank. In the end the *Banque de France* received around 130 tonnes, and thus recovered two-thirds of the gold which it had lost.

On 22 June the French cruiser *Emile Bertin* left Halifax for Fort de France, with the 300 tons of gold that she had brought from Brest.

Camille Huysmans was a prominent Belgian socialist, who had been mayor of Antwerp. On June 20 1940, he escaped through Bayonne on the *Leopold II*, a Belgian cargo ship; one of many not listed as taking part in Operation Aerial. When he arrived at Falmouth he was refused permission to land, until Deputy Prime Minister Clement Attlee intervened with a telegram.

On June 27th, he arrived in London where he stayed throughout the war. He also made efforts to build up a diamond industry in England with workers rom Antwerp. His intention was that this industry would go back to Antwerp after the war.

Probably the most dramatic salvage carried out at that time was by another collier, the Polish *Chorzow*, of only 845 gross registered tons. *Chorzow* had carried coal or tar to Bordeaux where she was requisitioned to help with the evacuation. She embarked 193 Polish airmen, who wanted to join their squadron at Northolt.

One of those who boarded was not an aviator; Dr. Karol Estreicher's mission was to escort the Polish National Treasure to Britain. The treasure had already been on an epic journey by barge, horse and cart, bus and lorry to Romania were it was taken aboard a merchant ship. The ship was twice intercepted by the Royal Navy, who suspected that she was carrying cargo for the enemy: on the second occasion she was escorted into Malta to be searched. From there she went to Genoa. The priceless cargo was then taken to Marseilles and then on to Aubusson, where it was stored for four months.

On 19 May the custodians decided that France was no longer safe and the treasure resumed its journey; this time to Bordeaux. At Bordeaux Polkowski and Zaleski (?) drove their lorry to the Polish consulate, there they explained their needs. Staff at the consulate told them that the only Polish ship in the port was the small coaster *Chorzow*, commanded by a Captain Gora.

When Gora arrived, he listened to the Consul's story and, without a word, climbed into the cab of the lorry and guided the lorry to the port. As they approached the dock gate he told the driver to 'put his foot down' and they swept pass the shouting security guards. When they reached the ship the crew were told to transfer the treasure into the hold as quickly as they could.

By the time the guards arrived the lorry had been unloaded and the lorry crew were hidden on board the ship. When the Master was asked why he had not stopped at the dock gate he said that he saw no reason to, as the lorry was empty. He then sent them off as he 'had more important things to do.'

The *Chorzow* sailed from Le Verdon on the same day as the *Broompark*. She was probably in the convoy that was astern of the *Broompark*, but, when one of the other ships was hit by a bomb, she went on to Falmouth alone also arriving on the 21st. From there the cargo was taken by rail to the Polish Embassy in London.

Later the treasure was carried to Canada by the Polish passenger liner *Batory;* reaching Halifax on the 12 July. At the time of the rescue from

France *Batory* and her sister ship *Sobieski* had been playing an important part in the Operation Aerial evacuation.

The Polish treasures were carefully packed in specialty constructed large trunks and long metal tubes. The consignment included:

'Szczerbiec', the jewelled Coronation sword of Polish Kings dating back to 1320, a two volume of Gutenberg Bible, 136 Flemish Tapestries some of which had been commissioned by King Sigjsmund III Augustus between 1549 and 1572, an aquamarine sceptre set in gold, the sword of the Order of the White Eagle and the Chain of the Order last used at the Coronation of King Stanislaw Augustus Poniatowskii in 1764, the Prayer Book of Queen Bona, religious manuscripts from the 13th century, the 14th century Florian Psalter - the oldest translation of the Psalms into Polish, the Annals of the Holy Cross, written by Archbishop Jacob of Znin in the early 13th century and thought to be the oldest preserved original Polish document, thirty six original Chopin compositions and thirteen pieces of his correspondence, hundreds of pieces of gold and silver cups and mugs, sabres, salvers, clocks and suits of armour from the 17th century and a chessboard belonging to King Sigismund III from 1608.

Much of the story is at the Polish Institute and Sikorski Museum in London. The *Chorzow*'s records are in archive A42, items 54 and 408. There do not seem to be CUST files at The National Archives referring to this shipment; the story is that the Poles just flatly refused to let Customs open the crates!

Myths

* Suffolk did not obtain the diamonds by raiding jewellers in Paris.

* Suffolk and Miss Morden did not cross France alone; they were in touch with Golding and Miss Nicolle, who helped them to get a lorry when their car was seized.

* It was not necessary to get the Master and his officers drunk to keep them in port: the ship's officers knew far better than others the hazards that awaited them at sea and Captain Paulsen was a teetotaller. A crew of about twenty would have been needed, just to get the ship to sea.

* The cargo was not 'left in a cave' to be collected and brought back to the UK by a warship or a submarine.

* Suffolk did not have to talk his way into the Ministry of Supply when he returned to London, he was expected and arrived with the DSR. He always signed himself 'Suffolk and Berkshire' (or on one occasion S & B), not just 'Suffolk'.

* No destroyer was sent to pick up Bichelonne and the others, though hurried messages were sent about their whereabouts after a twenty four hours delay.

Bibliography/Sources

Primary

The National Archives: AVIA 22/2288A, AVIA 22/3201 & CUST 106/884; BT 381/1672, the Official Log and Articles of Agreement of the *Broompark*.

Communications log for Operation Aerial*

Ian Golding, his father's records, through ww2talk.com/forum and direct, Including Marguerite Nicolle's diary – from Paris 10 June, to 8 July *

Dr Don Cody, material about his grandfather Captain Olaf Paulsen

Denholm Lines, they lost many records when their offices were bombed.

Oral History Transcript - Dr Lew Kowarski 1959?

Hubert (later Baron) Ansiaux - *Souvenirs*

Paul Timbal *Diamond Odyssey*, included in: *Financing the World's Most Precious Treasures* by Bruno Comer and Chaim Even-Zohar. 2009.

P. Timbal, *Why the Belgian Diamonds never Fell into the En+emy Hands.* – by Bruno Comer. Commission Royal Histoire ISBN 978-2-87044-007-0

The archives of the Antwerp Diamond Bank, Belgium. So far unpublished

Much of the story of the Polish treasure is at the Polish Institute and Sikorski Museum in London. The *Chorzow*'s records are in archive A42, items 54 and 408. There do not seem to be CUST files at The National Archives referring to this shipment.

IWM 99/37/1, Escape from Bordeaux, Andrew Miss R 10 pages.
IWM 07/20/1, Escape from France in 1940, Blunt Lt C E 9 pages

   *   *Among appendices to print edition only.*

Secondary

http://trove.nla.gov.au/newspaper/result?q=Earl+of+Suffolk. Various references to the Earl, his visit on the *Mount Stewart*, his return to Australia and his long stay there, his 1935 illness and his appointment in Paris.

Earl Raided Bank Vaults, Foiled Invading Germans, Sunday Dispatch, 23 May 1942

The Saturday Evening Post 28 November 1942 – not seen. Writing about this article the Suffolk family solicitor says 'It is unnecessary for me to comment on the vulgar style of the article.' (Also referred to in a letter from Captain Paulsen to his family 4 December 1942)

The Incredible Earl of Suffolk. Reader's Digest in April 1943.

La Bataille de L'Eau Lourde. Broompark, 1948 many websites

www.radley.org.uk/OR/OldRadleian/2009/PDFs/7%20Incredible%20Earl%20of%20Suffolk.pdf Reprint of *The Sunday Dispatch* 1942

My Elizabethan Brother, the Earl of Suffolk by Greville Howard, *Reader's Digest* 1969

The Race for Norwegian Heavy Water, 1940-1945, IFS Info 4/1995
Particularly Bertrand Goldschmidt pages 17 – 26.

The scruffy earl who swung the war, James Owen Daily Telegraph 24 June 2010

The Dragon's Opponent. BBC TV series 1973. (Episode 3)

Later films about sites in this story:

The Heroes of Telemark - the later raid on the plant at Ryukan.

The Cockleshell Heroes - the later raid on Bordeaux shipping by the SBS.

The Use of Heavy Water as a Moderator

Before considering the use of heavy water as a moderator it is first necessary to define what is 'heavy water' and what is a 'moderator'. To do this we need to delve a bit into some basic science.

What is 'Heavy Water'

Hydrogen is the simplest of those elements that make up our known world. To generalize, all elements from the simplest, hydrogen, to the most complex such as uranium, are comprised of three basic particles; electrons, protons and neutrons. The nucleus is comprised of protons along with neutrons, which act as a sort of glue, helping to hold the nucleus together (hydrogen, however, is a special case, as the common isotope is comprised of a single proton and electron with no neutron; by contrast uranium has 92 protons and almost 150 neutrons).

Protons have positive electrical charges, which are balanced by the negative charges of their accompanying electrons. Neutrons, as the name suggests, have no charge. One way the system can be visualized is as electrons orbiting around the central nucleus which is comprised of protons and neutrons. For a given element, the number of protons and electrons are fixed, but the number of neutrons varies; give or take a few.

As the chemical characteristics of an element depend on electron behaviour, the addition or subtraction of neutrons from the nucleus does not change its chemical properties, that is, a chemical element is defined by the number of protons in the nucleus (the Atomic Number). But the number of neutrons in the nucleus does change the Atomic Weight, which will alter various physical properties. These chemical elements, with varying numbers of neutrons in the nucleus, are called isotopes. So it follows that isotopes of the same element cannot be separated by chemical means and separation must be carried out using physical processes.

In the case of hydrogen there are three isotopes; 'hydrogen' with one proton, 'deuterium' with one proton and one neutron and the unstable isotope, radioactive 'tritium' with one proton and two neutrons. But all three of these hydrogen isotopes possess a single proton and therefore they all behave chemically as hydrogen and only differ in their physical properties. Note that hydrogen is almost unique amongst the elements in having individual names for its three isotopes (an exception that springs to mind is radon and thoron, both isotopes of the inert radioactive gas radon).

Water (H_2O) is comprised of two atoms of hydrogen combined with one atom of oxygen. Natural water contains 0.0145% of heavy water (deuterium oxide - D_2O) or approximately one part in 5,000. Heavy water is separated from natural water using various physical means. The heavy water produced during the war at Telemark in Norway was a by-product of hydrogen generation (the hydrogen was produced by the electrolysis of water using relatively cheap hydroelectric power and converted to ammonia for fertilizer manufacture). The separation process is slow and expensive, for example the plant at Vermark produced 12 metric tonnes per year at peak production; typically one litre of D_2O from 325 tonnes of water.

Note that a modern-day Canadian CANDU reactor requires an inventory of some 500 tonnes of heavy water and an annual make-up of approximately 20 tonnes to compensate for leakage. It should also be noted that D_2O is not a component of a basic fission bomb. It is, however, an important material as a precursor in the production of plutonium, one of the two fissionable bomb materials used by the USA at the end of the war. And, incidentally, it is a fuel component of the fusion, or hydrogen, bomb – but that's another story!

Moderators and Nuclear Fission

To understand the importance of heavy water and its production in those dark days of 1940 it is also necessary to delve a bit deeper into the principles of nuclear fission. Fission occurs with certain large, unstable elements, such as uranium and plutonium, with the release of large amounts of energy, excess neutrons and two 'fission products' (each of approximately half the size of the original element). The excess neutrons released can cause fission in further atoms of fissionable material and under the right conditions a chain reaction will occur. Typically, between two and three neutrons are released per atom when fission occurs.

In the early days it was recognized that there could be two routes to a fission bomb - via the fissionable isotopes uranium-235 and man-made plutonium-239. But because of early uncertainties the Allies, in the Manhattan Project, decided it was essential to pursue both options, i.e. to produce high purity kilogram quantities of the two fissionable isotopes U-235 and Pu-239.

Natural uranium, as it occurs in mineral deposits throughout the world, consists of approximately 0.7% fissionable U-235 and the remainder non-fissionable U-238, so to make a uranium bomb it is necessary to physically separate the two uranium isotopes – an extremely difficult physical process because their atomic weights are so similar (235 and 238). Hence the huge uranium hexafluoride, gaseous diffusion plants which were built in the States to produce weapons grade uranium (i.e. approximately 90% U-235).

Obtaining plutonium for the second option was almost as difficult, as it was a by-product of reactor operations fuelled with natural uranium. It was produced by building a 'pile' containing natural uranium (because enriched uranium or pure U-235 was not available at that stage). Simply building a pile containing natural uranium will do nothing because the spare neutrons from U-235 fission will simply be absorbed by the U-238. But if the fast neutrons, resulting from fission, can be slowed to thermal energies they are no longer captured to the same extent by U-238 and a self-maintaining chain reaction can be obtained.

To slow down the fast neutrons the ideal material (known as a 'moderator') is a low atomic weight element (or a compound) that the neutrons can bounce around in, losing their energy but without being captured (paradoxically, one of the best light elements for absorbing neutrons is boron and hence its use in control and shutdown rods).

The most suitable moderating materials are those containing hydrogen, carbon and beryllium. The latter is no longer used because of its high cost and toxicity, so that leaves hydrogen and carbon.

Once the pile is operational neutrons will still be lost into the U-238, but not enough to stop a chain reaction as long as the pile is big enough (hundreds of tons of fuel and moderator are necessary; ruling out its use as a bomb). Those neutrons which react with the U-238 form the man-made element Pu-239 (by transmutation via short-lived neptunium - U-238 + n > Np-239 > Pu-239). So to make a plutonium bomb it is necessary to separate this element from the used fuel. This can be carried out by chemical processing, so theoretically it is much easier than U-235 separation, but unfortunately it's intensely radioactive at this stage, requiring heavy shielding and remote operations. It was, however, a more compact and predictable route to a bomb.

Returning to moderators, water is a good material but unless you have slightly enriched uranium it absorbs too many neutrons (forming deuterium oxide and eventually tritium oxide) to be effective. However, if one can use D_2O (or pure graphite) as moderator it is much more effective – D_2O will still absorb neutrons to form tritium oxide, which is radioactive with a 12 year half-life, but it becomes possible to use natural uranium as fuel.

Significance to WW2 and Germany

The Germans realised it would be impractical to separate uranium isotopes with their resources - especially during a war. So they were aiming for the more compact plutonium option and hence their interest in heavy water, as they didn't have the facilities to produce large quantities of high purity graphite. They also had the disadvantage that many of their physicists had left the country, ending up in the USA via the UK. The fascists had expelled many of these from the German technical institutes due to their being of Jewish extraction; the most well-known of these of course was Albert Einstein.

With D_2O moderated reactors, apart from the initial capital cost, the main problem is one of radioactive tritium and tritiated water release produced by the neutron absorption of heavy water.

Terence Holland, January 2014

Appendix Two

The Suffolk/Golding report dated 25 June 1940

On Saturday, the 15th June, after consultation with Major Golding, we decided that the situation was sufficiently grave to necessitate our proceeding to Bordeaux. Having done so we reported to the Ministere of Armament at 56, rue Commondant Arnould, where we assisted at a Meeting with Monsieur Dautry, then the Minister of Armament.

In view of the gravity of the situation Monsieur Dautry decided to save everything he could from the clutches of the Germans and he decided to send two Missions, which had been composed by General Martignon and General Blanchard, to the U.S.A.

In the course of the conversation with Monsieur Dautry we ascertained that the Ministry of Supply was in urgent need of technicians. Since telephonic and postal communications were in a state of the most utter chaos there was no possible chance of confirming this with the Ministry, so we decided to proceed upon our own initiative. We therefore requested of Monsieur Dautry as many armament experts and scientists as he could spare, which he gladly and willingly accorded to us, at the same time giving us as many machine tools as we could take away in the ship. He then instructed Captain Bichelonne, his Chef du Cabinet Technique, to facilitate and expedite these arrangements to the best of his ability, which Captain Bichelonne did.

On the Sunday evening, however, the Reynaud Cabinet at last fell and the acts of Monsieur Dautry were, in fact, null. In despite of this, however, we proceeded to gather together as many armament experts and scientists as we possibly could, still aided by Captain Bichelonne, and we commenced the loading of the machine tools.

We should at this juncture like to mention that until representations were made by one of us, i.e. Lord Suffolk, to the highest quarter and in the most uncompromising and bald terms had been made, we met with nothing but the most obstructive and defeatist attitude from the higher members of the Bordeaux Government. However, the demands to Marshall Petain having been made, we succeeded in extracting from him permission to embark the technicians and scientists which we had brought with us.

We then set about acquiring a ship, which said ship was made available to us by the British Embassy through its Commercial Attache, Mr. Irving, the said ship being the s.s."Broompark", of Denham Ltd. (Denholm) of Glasgow, captained by Captain Paulsen.

By Tuesday morning it was obvious that our presence in Bordeaux was known to the 5th Column, since there had been an attempt, which was fortunately unsuccessful, to bomb our ship. However we proceeded loading machine tools until five o'clock on Wednesday morning, when we decided that, for the safety of what we had already carried it would be as well to weigh anchor and sail for home.

Exclusive of the cargo of machine tools and eminent scientists and armament personnel we had been entrusted by Mr. Irving with the carrying of a parcel containing over £3,000,000 worth of diamonds, together with three gentlemen in whose custody this consignment was put. This consignment was sought by the Ministry of Economic Warfare.

Additional to the above cargo we also carried the entire world stock of the commodity known as "heavy water" (to wit, deuterium oxide, D_2O), together with two members of Professor Curie's Laboratory, who were competent to carry on an extremely important research to which this invaluable commodity was essential.

We also succeeded in extracting from the Naval Authorities in Bordeaux two anti-aircraft '75' mm. guns, one "under and over" 9mm pair of Hotchkiss machine guns and one single barrelled Hotchkiss anti-aircraft machine gun of the same calibre.

We also succeeded in securing a gun crew of picked members of the French Navy, especially skilled in anti-aircraft defence.

As previously stated we weighed anchor at five o'clock on Wednesday morning and proceeded to Le Verdon at the mouth of the Gironde, where we took on ammunition for the anti-aircraft equipment, and where we also made one final effort to collect more scientific personnel. This having been done we set sail for Falmouth and arrived there at 8 a.m. on Friday morning, where we communicated with the Ministry of Supply and having cleared our personnel through the formalities of immigration and Customs we landed them, together with the diamonds, the various secret papers belonging to various members of the Mission and our own, and the "heavy water" under a guard furnished by the Military Authorities of Falmouth. We then procured a special train, loaded such onto this and proceeded to London, where we arrived at 10 a.m. on the Saturday morning. The personnel of armament experts and scientists were then bestowed in the Great Western Hotel and the diamonds delivered to the offices of the Diamond Corporation whilst the papers and the "heavy water" proceeded, under guard, to a place of security, i.e. Wormwood Scrubs.

We should like to make this the occasion of expressing our warmest thanks to the following people:-

Captain Bichelonne and Colonel Raguet of the Ministere de l'Armament, without whose devoted help, without whose unparalleled efficiency and without whose heartfelt sympathies our mission could not even have started.

To the members of the British Embassy who were at that time in Bordeaux, with especial reference to the Commercial Attache, Mr Irving, and the Minister, Mr Harvey, who in the case of Mr Irving secured us our ship, and in the case of Mr Harvey secured us an omnibus passport and clearance through the Customs, without which our task would have been made immeasurably more arduous and difficult.

To Captain Paulsen, the Officers and members of the ship's crew of the s.s. Broompark, who afforded the most loyal, painstaking and hardworking assistance to us and who, in circumstances which might have been of extreme discomfort, did all they could to make us and our personnel as comfortable as circumstances would allow.

Thanks are also due to Mr Barton, who was a Director of the International Chamber of Commerce in Paris, and whom the Embassy asked us to transport as a passenger. Mr Barton took endless trouble to organise the catering department of our journey on the ship and did this very successfully.

Also our thanks are due to Monsieur Berthiez, who when we were faced with the removal of our dock foreman and dockers organised a scratch crew from the Port and with the aid of the 1st Mate of the ship and Colonel Liebessart, superintended the extremely difficult matter of loading these machine tools himself.

We should also like to comment most favourably upon the efficiency, courtesy and diligence shown to us by Lt. Commdr. Mills, R.N.V.R., of the Falmouth Contraband Control. This Officer did everything within his power to facilitate the landing and despatch of our personnel and valuables and was of the very greatest possible assistance to us.

Finally, we should like to cite in the very warmest manner possible the conduct of our two secretaries, Miss Morden and Miss Nicolle. Faced with the most uncomfortable possible conditions, faced with hours of work which frequently amounted to some twenty per day, faced at times with the greatest possible danger, they conducted themselves coolly, calmly and extremely efficiently and did what they could to render the operation a success.

TNA File

Marguerite Nicolle: Notes on our Flight from France.

Monday June 10th, 1940.

Major Golding calls me at 11.30 p.m. instead of at 4 a.m. as originally planned. This means things are hot. Make a call at A.P.M. and M.A. where we collect Miss Bruneau's luggage and canaries. (Miss Bruneau formed part of the M.A. Staff but was unable to get near her station on account of the fearful crowds and so missed her train). Called for Mrs. Morrison who wants to return to England via St. Malo.

Finally leave Paris by the Porte de Versailles about an hour or so before the arrival of the Germans. Our progress on the road is necessarily very slow as we are continually held up by military convoys, lorries and war material which seem to go both ways. We are caught in an air raid just on the outskirts of Paris. We drive without lights and in a thick mist (I was told afterwards that this mist was artificially created by the Germans to hide their progress but don't know how true this is). We drive non-stop until dawn.

Tuesday June 11th, 1940.

3.30 a.m. Dawn is breaking and Maj. Golding calls a halt to snatch a little sleep. After an attempt at half and hour's sleep sitting up in the car, packed to the top with all our luggage and office papers, we continue on our route towards Orleans. With the break of day appear refugees from everywhere – lorries and cars of every description are now on the road and we can't get along in spite of the fact that we have a military car and Maj. Golding shouts at all the agents "Mission Militaire". We are compelled to take the side roads and go a little out of our way but gain in the long run judging from the time other people took to reach Orleans.

<u>We arrive at Orleans at 9 a.m.</u> and go straight to the Military Barracks to replenish in petrol. Then to an hotel to try and get something to eat. Manage to get tea and "biscottes" but no bread available.

Here we run into Mrs. MacDonald of the M.T.C. Major Golding goes to her assistance as she is stuck for petrol. Continue on our way towards Tours. We go via Blois, (Chateaux de la Loire district) Beautiful country and lovely weather.

<u>Reach Tours at 1.30 p.m.</u> Immediately on our arrival we run into Maj. Witterington. While Maj. Golding and he confer in the car, we, all the womenfolk hunt around for something to eat. We succeed in finding a restaurant that still has something left as the town is absolutely empty of food on account of the hundreds of thousands of refugees there. Bring sandwiches back for Maj. Golding, and we try to make our way towards the British Consulate. It takes about ½ an hr. to cross the bridge at Tours the traffic is so dense and has got blocked. Maj. Golding gets out and does policemen and we finally move on. When on the other side of the bridge we find no Br. Consulate – we have been wrongly directed and have to make our way back again over the bridge. This again takes us some time. Get Mrs. Morrison fixed up at the Consulate with a car for Le Mans where she can make her way to St. Malo. Miss Bruneau stays as this is where her office is installed and she runs into her boss so we leave her happy.

It is now about 5 p.m. Maj. Golding & I are now the only ones left and we drive to the Chateau at Clerc a few miles outside Tours to make contact with the Embassy and M.A. Return to Tours at 7.30 p.m. At the embassy we meet the M.T.C. (Mrs. MacDonald and her girls). Decide to stay in Tours for the night and Maj. Golding leaves me to watch over the car while he and Mrs. MacDonald look for rooms. After sitting 2-½ hours in the car I am beginning to despair when they return and have worked the miracle of finding two rooms for the lot of us. This is really marvellous in view of the thousands of refugees in Tours.

We have a jolly reunion at the Hotel Univers in spite of feeling desperately dirty and tired. Here we meet Mr. Metcalfe who has been shot down by the R.A.F. on his way back to England by plane. He has a miraculous escape and entertains us with his adventures. He is by no means downhearted but would like to get back all the same. Everything he possessed was burnt in the plane. We separate to sleep and arrange to meet the following morning at 10 a.m. at the Hotel Univers. Air raid.

Wednesday 12th June, 1940

10 a.m. we all meet again at the Hotel Univers. We who have managed to sleep feel very refreshed in spite of nightmares and alarm clocks going off, but Maj. Golding doesn't feel quite so fresh having slept the night in the car and he gets let down over the shaving business in the morning!

We go round to the Prefecture and get the Mechanised Transport Corps fixed up with more petrol and here we say good-bye to them. Mr. Metcalfe stays behind with Maj. Golding and myself and we go back to Orleans neighbourhood to get him on a plane to England. We make various visits to various R.A.F. quarters where Maj. Golding fixes the whole thing up for Mr. Metcalfe and we manage to get a very good lunch at the R.A.F. Mess. I omitted to mention that we had a puncture on the way: - our first!

We see Mr. Metcalfe off at about 5 p.m. (Must say that I have much admired the R.A.F.'s various quarters – they have an eye to beauty). We now continue our journey to Mont Dore via Bourges, where we stop to have dinner at about 8.30 p.m. Try to get rooms for the night as Maj. Golding is too tired to go on driving and we can't possibly make it. Not a room to be had so we drive on to a little village called St. Amand *(St. Armand – Montrond?)* and try there. No better luck – full of refugees from everywhere and not a bed to be had. Maj. Golding gets a brilliant idea. Are there any chateaux about? Yes, we are told and directed to the Chateaux de …. Owned by the Vicomtesse de …… We'll try and get you put up says Maj. Golding and I'l *(sic)* sleep in the car. We knock up the people at the chateau. (real castle of olden days) Ring a clanging bell which is eventually answered – ensures conversation between closed door, afterwards opened, bringing to our view a young woman and a monk. This is a bit of a surprise. We apologise, explain, and ask to be put up. Most suspicious at first but although we might look tired and dirty we don't look too villainous (secret congratulations on our faces) and they decide to let us in. When confidence is completely installed I get a bed in the hall and Maj. Golding gets a mattress as there wasn't another bed. They 'phoned the police and while the beds are being prepared we catch them out telling the police that we are quite all right. Their turn to apologise and we see the joke. Very hospital *(sic)* people – give us wine and biscuits after which we all retire until morning. (In this particular castle were nuns and school children refugees from the Metz district). <u>In the morning</u> we are woken by the padre who entertains us at breakfast and we have to produce our papers in view of the police episode of the night before. The Vicomtesse is perfectly charming and speaks quite good English. We bid her farewell and promise to call and see her again if we are ever in the vicinity again. (I believe this is still the unoccupied area).

Friday 14th June

Start about business in the office but already there are funny rumours running around. Have to fight to keep our car and get petrol coupons for Maj. Golding's proposed trip to Paris, Limoges etc… Empty the town of Michelin maps. Cold and rainy. Work until 9 p.m. and leave Maj. Golding who plans to leave at dawn the following morning on his trip.

Saturday 15th June

8.30 a.m. A knock at the door. It's Major Golding. "Thought you had gone" I say. "No, things aren't so good and we might have to leave for Bordeaux to-day" he replies. "Be packed and at the office in ten minutes". I turn up at the office a few minutes later to find everything and everybody gone – just disappeared. Catch a glimpse of Cmdt. Brière who is more hot and bothered than usual and frightfully excited. I ask what is happening but he is quite incoherent. I await Maj. Golding who comes along with Lord Suffolk. They decide that we should leave. Again we load the car and once again I keep watch while Maj. Golding does business. While waiting and watching who do I see go by – Charles Berthiez. I tap the window to draw his attention – he is delighted to see me because he knows that Maj. Golding can't be far off. I tell him to stick with me and they'll meet. Maj. Golding returns at about 12 and talks with Mr. Berthiez. It is arranged that Mr. Berthiez will take over Maj. Golding's room. There is more running around and as it is now gone 1.30 we decide to have something to eat before leaving. The four of us, Maj. Golding, Mr.

Berthiez, his assistant and myself have lunch together at the Mess. Afterwards there are more things to settle up and finally we are about to leave when Maj. Golding catches sight of the wooden case just arrived from Paris and feared lost, containing all our office files. We empty the contents into a suitcase which we put in the car. It is now about 5 p.m. and this time we really do leave Mont Dore. Passing by Bourboulle we stop to see how Lord Suffolk is getting along and find that his car has been taken from him and he can't get away. We return to Mont Dore and where Maj. Golding gets him fixed up with a lorry in which he piles all his luggage and travels to Bordeaux with Miss Morden in this conveyance. Once again Maj. Golding and I start out with the chauffeur Bloch squashed in at the back of the car almost smothered with luggage. We drive through a very lovely part of France known as the Massif Central. The weather is glorious. We pass through Tulle, Perigueux, Libourne. At Perigueux Maj. Golding calls a halt and we try to trace an English nurse, who, however, has already left. On the way we discover our spare tyre is flat and we try to get it arranged but it is already gone 8 p.m. and we can find no place. Eventually on the road, a long way from any town, we find a kind of repair shop and they attend to it. While the repair is being effected Maj. Golding puts a call through to Limoges and we partake of sandwiches brought along with us, together with some juicy "plums" – sticky but nice. After that we just drive on. There is quite a fog, we have to change our lights. Bloch takes over the wheel as Maj. Golding is just dropping. However after a few hours Bloch appears to be falling asleep so Maj. Golding takes it over again and we reach Bordeaux at about 2 a.m. Sunday morning. There is the usual air raid on and the 'agent' on the far side of the bridge yells at us. We are stopped for papers (this is about the 100th time since our departure).

Sunday 16th June 2.a.m.

Bordeaux is absolutely blacked-out and none of us know why. Nobody is about and we find difficulty in finding the Prefecture. We run into a lorry driver who comes to our aid and guides us to the Prefecture. Here they won't let Maj. Golding in and we get sent some other place in town. Here we are sent back to the first place. This time they let Maj. Golding in and after an absence of about half an hour he returns with letters enabling us to put up at the Chapon Fin Hotel in the rooms reserved for the Minister and his Secretary. It is now gone 3 a.m. and we retire to bed. At 8.30 we are about again. Meantime Lord Suffolk and Miss Morden arrived (at 6.30 a.m.). Miss Morden and I are given the day off until 6 p.m. We rest in the morning and go around the town to find some place to lunch but there are literally millions of people at Bordeaux and this is impossible, so we return to the hotel and lunch there where we are joined by Lord Suffolk and Maj. Golding. (I forgot to mention that during the morning, the shops being open until 12, I was commissioned to buy a suit case for Lord Suffolk who just didn't know where to put his things. This was an awful business as a large size suit case was the hardest thing to buy in Bordeaux. After trying at least six shops I found something suitable). At 6 p.m. we are awaiting our respective bosses when Mr. Berthiez arrives. Lord Suffolk and Maj. Golding return at about 7.30 with the news that we must go on board some boat that night. Then follows a lot of rushing around, visits to the Ministère de l'Armement premises, the Br. Consulate, packing up of the lorry to take all our luggage down to the port where it is loaded on the s/s BROOMPARK, a coal boat on which we are to cross over to England. The chauffeur Bloch is very upset because he can't dine with his wife who came all the way from Mont Dore. We return to the Chapon Fin to have dinner then the two Berthiez, Miss Morden and myself take possession of our quarters on the boat which was to be our home for nearly a week. We all go to bed. Lord Suffolk and Maj. Golding return to the hotel.

Monday 17th June

The next day we see little of our bosses. They are running around Bordeaux on business. Mme. Berthiez, Miss Morden and myself are told not to leave the boat. We try to rest but can't as we are all worked up. We hear of machinery which is to be salvaged, rumours that the French Govt. has capitulated but as far as we are concerned a quiet day. At night we retire to our bunks after listening to the Captain's funny stories. In the middle of the night we are told to get up as the port is being bombed by the Germans. Col. Liebesart is now on board. The boat is also being loaded, and provisions and blankets for the mission are being brought on board also. There is great activity on board as the boat is being loaded. We go from one wharf to another picking up this enormous cargo. Rumours still high. We see little of our bosses. Stray passengers are beginning to come on board and I hear that it is the Captain's intention to take 500 refugees on board. I feel the bosses should be informed of this. Mme. Berthiez drives the car bringing Col. Liebesart and myself to Bordeaux to look for Maj. Golding and Lord Suffolk. We go to the Br. Consulate and find huge crowds outside waving passports (the British ones). The Consulate is rushed off its feet and chaos reigns. We don't find Maj. Golding and proceed to the Chapon Fin to see if he is at his hotel. No luck; we go to the restaurant – no luck. We have a breakdown, the car gets stuck in the middle of the road. We manage to push it to the side and leave Mme. Berthiez to look after it while the Col. And myself get a lift in a private car which takes us to the Ministère de l'Armement. Here we finally run both Maj. Golding and Lord Suffolk down. They are arranging the Mission. It is now about 2.30 p.m. Tell them the tale and the go round to the Naval Attaché to fix the matter up. We go from one place to another and at about 4.30 p.m. return to the boat. There are quite a number of people on board and Miss Morden and I are kept very busy attending to them. The boat is still being loaded. In the evening it rains hard. All the crew seem to be on shore and the loaders turn up asking for Mr. Berthiez who is nowhere to be seen. It is very dark, the R.A.F. are on board – men turn up with the guns and others to fix them and there is nobody except the 2nd mate. Streams of Poles and Belgians arrive some with passes others without – they all want to get on board. Members of the Mission turn up. They expect to find bunks, i.e. proper accommodation and food. I have to disillusion them and give out blankets. All this goes on for about 2 hrs, when at midnight to my great relief Mr. Berthiez turns up, followed shortly by Lord Suffolk. Maj. Golding and Mr. Berthiez attend to the loading while we attend to the passengers. (Miss Morden and myself). Lord Suffolk is buzzing around doing all kinds of things. And so the night goes on.

Wednesday 19[th.]

We leave Bordeaux at 6 a.m. After getting about half way up the river we are held up. A boat in front of us has struck a mine. There are more than a thousand passengers on board but all are saved except those killed in the explosion. The boat takes nearly two hours to sink and then there is nothing left of her except floating wreckage. No sign of a boat ever having been there. The boat was a French boat. After this interruption we go slowly out of Bordeaux not feeling so bright. The next thing is to arrange for meals & lifeboat accommodation in the event of being torpedoed. This is no small matter. We are about 110 on board and hardly any of them have brought anything with them.

Thursday 20th June

We are kept very busy. We have an Air raid warning and all gone down into the hold. Nothing happens. We are not convoyed and it appears we had to dodge submarines. Not enough lifebelts so make inner tubes of cars into lifebelts for the men.

Friday 21st June.

We reach Falmouth safely at about six a.m. The authorities come on board. We serve our last meal to all the passengers as it has been decided that we shall stay the night in Falmouth. The day is spent, (i.e. the afternoon) in collecting all the blankets, enamel plates, forks, knives, etc. which were loaned to the passengers. We also collect the inner tubes belonging to the various cars on board. At about 8.30 p.m. the passport authorities come on board. I am collared to assist them and spend from then until midnight going through the passports and filling out immigration forms. It is raining and when I come out of the dining room where the passport officials were working I find myself stranded with part of the luggage and all of our party gone. Fortunately an officer who had just left Maj. Golding tells me where I can find him and I get taken round. I here learn that Maj. Golding had been looking for me for quite a while. I get carried off to some Club and provided with sandwiches and a whisky. Then go back and with Maj. Golding go to board the train. Plans were changed and we are going straight to London. Maj. Golding and I have a compartment to ourselves and manage to sleep a little.

Saturday 22ⁿᵈ June

We reach Paddington at 9 a.m. A breakfast is awaiting our party at the G.W.R. Hotel where we all adjourn. Accommodation is arranged for our party at the hotel and Miss Morden and I wait for our respective bosses. We wait until 4 p.m. then Lord Suffolk appears. He goes off for the weekend and I wait for Maj. Golding. At 7 p.m. I'm wondering what has happened and decide whatever happens to take a room at the hotel. It is then that I discover that Maj. Golding telephoned at about 5 p.m. I get in touch with him. I remain at the hotel until Tuesday looking after the Mission.

Appendix Four

The Suffolk/Golding party:

Colonel LIBESSART	Applied Physics, ballistics
Prof. & Mdm. CORDIER	Both Physiologists
Colonel & Mdm. L'HOMME & 3 children	Ballistics & weapons
M. LAUDENBACH	Tank production specialist
Mdm. HAURIE (ORY?)	Secretary Col. L'Homme
Colonel MARTIN-PREVEL	Armoured vehicles
Capt. & Mdm. DARMOIS*	Mathematician
Prof. MILLOT*	Biologist
Colonel de SAINT PAUL	Armoured vehicles
M. LUCE	Engineer
Prof. & Mdm. GALLIOT & 2 children	Inventor, Armaments
Dr. & Mdm. MASSENAUD & 1 child	Powder Engineer
M. & Mdm. PASCAL & 1 child	Dr. Massenaud's team
M. ENDERLIN & sister	Dr. Massenaud's team
M. PERIMUTTER & sister	Dr. Massenaud's team
Prof. CATHALA	Best Organic Chemist
Dr. LE GUYON*	Bacteriologist
Dr. FAGUET*	Physio-Chemistry
Prof. BARANGER	Bio & Organic Chemist
Brigadier MERCIER	Prof. Baranger's team
M. THOMAS	Prof. Baranger's team
M. CARTIER	Prof. Baranger's team
M. LACAZE	Prof. Baranger's team
Prof. LONGCHAMBON*	Minerologist
Mlle. LAPIERRE*	Longchambon's Secretary
Prof. LAUGIER	Physiologist
Dr. BOUTILLIER*	Civil Engineer Laugier
Dr. van ERMINGEN-DUWEZ (Belgian)	Physiologist & Surgeon
Colonel & Mdm. LAPAYRE & 2 children	
Dr. & Mdm. von HALBAN & 1 child	Prof Joliot-Curie's team
Dr. & Mdm. KOWARSKI & child	Prof Joliot-Curie's team
M. & Mdm. ANSIAUX (Belgians)	Antwerp Diamond Bank
M. & Mdm. MAYER (Belgians)	Mdm. Ansiaux's parents

M. & Mdm. WARNANT & child (Belgians) Commercial Engineer
M. & Mdm. BERTHIEZ   Machine tool factory

Returned to France on, or about, 19 July; some because they were not offered a suitable post and others because they were concerned for the safety of members of their family who remained in France.

Not part of Lord Suffolk's party:
M. GUERON   Chemist
M.DEVYS   Chemist
M. HIRSCH   Chemist
Mr & Mrs TIMBAL & 2 children   Antwerp Diamond Bank
Miss ALGOTSON (Swedish Nanny)   Mme. Timbal was Swedish
Mr & Mrs de HAAN
Mr van CAMPENHOUT

A list kept by Colonel Golding shows the following, with their wives where applicable, were authorized by the Ambassador to proceed to the UK:

Jean PANHARD   ]
M. DELAGUIERE   ]   PANHARD
M. CODILLOT   ]

BOULANGER   ]
M. LAMY   ]   CITROEN

M. GACHET   ]
M. CHEYSSON   ]
M. PERONI   ]   S.O.M.U.A.
M. DUCLOS   ]
M. HORET   ]
M. LAVIROTTE   ]
Ingr DEVENNE   ]   Ingénieurs Principaux
M. MARTIN-PREVEL]
Ing Prof ROLAND   ]   *in ink*

M. BIRKIGHT   ]   Hispano Suiza

124

Colonel St PAUL	]	
One BOURDAU	]	
Ingr Pal RICAUD	]	*No sponsor shown*
One PICARD	]	
M. HEURTAUX	]	RENAULT
M. MAGNE	]	Aviation

Only two of the above are in the first list

Five French gun's crew, one or more Polish officers, several British people remained in Falmouth.

Appendix Five

Operation Aerial Journal

(Provided by Don L Kindell)

Orders were given on June 15th for the withdrawal of the whole of The British Expeditionary Force from France, approximately 140,000 men

June 13th *BATORY, DUCHESS OF YORK, GEOGIC, SOBIESKI in convoy FF1, Clyde to Brest with French and Polish troops from the Norwegian Campaign. FF2, Clyde to St Nazaire: Ulster Monarch, Royal Ulsterman, Royal Scotsman and Ulster Prince[1]*

June 15th

EMPIRE ABILITY & CITY OF FLORENCE were ordered to sail from Falmouth to Brest, ETTRICK, KONINGIN EMMA, ROYAL ULSTERMAN & ROYAL SCOTSMAN to La Pallice CITY OFWINDSOR was diverted to Cherbourg from Convoy O.A.168 G.F. LANCASTRIA was ordered to proceed to Quiberon Bay for onward passage to St. Nazaire, and to Brest. ARANDORA STAR, OTRANTO & STRATHAIRD were ordered to Brest with all despatch from Cardiff, and ORMONDE & ORONSAY[2] from Falmouth to Quiberon Bay. HAVELOCK was ordered to detail one destroyer to escort the first loaded convoy.

O.I./C Southampton was ordered to sail CLEW BAY, KILRAE, AFON GWLI, HYTHE, WHITSTABLE, MALRIX, MARSWORTH & LYROCA & POLGRANGE to Quiberon Bay.

MACKAY & WINCHESLEA were ordered to sail to Brest at 0700/16 to escort loaded convoys to the United Kingdom.

D.S.T.O. Newhaven was ordered to sail FERMAIN, FIRECREST, NEPHRITE, OBSIDIAN & RAVONA to Brest with all despatch, and D.S.T.O. Shoreham was ordered to sail ARTHUR WRIGHT.

S.T.O. Avonmouth and S.T.O. Newport were ordered to sail CLAN FERGUSON, MARGOT, GOVERNOR & TEIRESIAS for St. with all despatch.

June 16th

Admiral Ouest was informed that EL KANTARA would sail for Brest pm. Sunday 16th June.

WOLVERINE, VANOC & WHIRLWIND were detailed to escort loaded ships to the United Kingdom.

---

[1] ***Items in italics are not part of the original document***

[2] ***Brest Arrivals**: Wed Jun 12, 1940, include BAHARISTAN; Fri Jun 14, 1940, CITY OF CHRISTCHURCH, **Sun Jun 16, 1940**, CITY OF FLORENCE, ETTRICK, ORMONDE, OTRANTO.   **Mon Jun 17, 1940**, CITY OF DERBY & STRATHAIRD, all independent; FRANCES DAWSON OA.168GF. **Brest Departures** CITY OF DERBY, BAHARISTAN, **Sat Jun 15, 1940**, BEURSPLEIN, CITY OF CHRISTCHURCH, PORT MONTREAL, YORKWOOD. **Sun Jun 16, 1940**, BLAIRANGUS, CANTERBURY, LADY OF MANN, ORMONDE, OTRANTO, VIENNA. **Mon Jun 17, 1940** CITY OF DERBY, KONINGIN EMMA, LYCAON, STRATHAIRD, ULSTER MONARCH. **Tue Jun 18, 1940** ETTRICK, CITY OF FLORENCE, **Wed Jun 19, 1940** JAMES MCGEE, Escorted, ATHELCHIEF. **Thu Jun 20, 1940** ANASTASSIA, DAVANGER, **Fri Jun 21, 1940**, FRANCES DAWSON. **Sat Jun 22, 1940**, VILJA*

FIRECREST, NEPHRITE, who had now arrived at Plymouth were ordered to remain there at short notice pending further orders, and S.T.O. Newhaven was ordered to sail FERMAIN for Plymouth forthwith.

MACKAY & WINCHESLEA sailed for Brest.

S.N.O. Brest reported that LADY OF MANN, MANXMAN & CANTERBURY were loaded with 6000 troops, but held up by mines. He intended to load VIENNA, who was in harbour under orders for Nantes.

B.N.L.O. Brest reported that more ships were urgently required at St. Nazaire. GEORGIC, DUCHESS OF YORK & SOBIESKI were to be loaded by dark and sailed, and BATORY was to be sailed at daylight on the following day. 13000 troops would be embarked, leaving 35000 there.

S.T.O. Plymouth was ordered to sail DAGMAR, MURAYFIELD, HYTHE, WHITSTABLE, YEWPARK, BETTSWORTH, NEPHRITE, MALRIX, MARSWORTH & FIRECREST to Qiberon Bay.

S.N.O. St. Nazaire was informed that GEORGIC & DUCHESS OF YORK were to be sailed for Liverpool when loaded and BATORY & SOBIESKI to Plymouth.

WESTCOTT was ordered to proceed to St. Nazaire to act under orders of Captain D.9.

Admiral Ouest was asked to sail ROYAL SCOTSMAN & ROYAL ULSTERMAN as soon as possible to Loire where they were urgently required to embark personnel.

ETTRICK, KONINGIN EMMA & LADY OF MANN were also to proceed to Quiberon Bay to embark troops from Loire. MACKAY was ordered to send destroyers not immediately required to join Captain D.9 at St, Nazaire. WESTCOTT was to join them on the following morning.

SUFFOLK COAST & ST. ANDREW sailed from Plymouth. HANTONIA & ST, BRIAC sailed 1815 from Southampton.

VANOC was ordered to St. Nazaire with all despatch, and HIGHLANDER also sailed for St. Nazaire.

ROBERT PROCIS, STARLING & BARON OGILVY sailed from Nantes for Milford Haven.

The trawlers CAPE MARIATO, BLIGHTY, MURMANSK, LACERTA, LOMBARD, WELBECK, & FLORIO all sailed from Plymouth for Brest.

D.S.T.O. Avonmouth and Falmouth were ordered to sail TRELAWNY, BRITANNY, CITY OF EVANSVILLE and PORT MONTREAL for Loire via Quiberon Bay a.m. June 17th.

At the end of June 16th the position was that 11000 troops had been embarked at St Malo, leaving 5000 there. 10,500 had embarked at Brest, leaving 16000 there. 17,000 had embarked at St. Nazaire, leaving 30000 there. The embarkation at Nantes was proceeding satisfactorily.

June 17th

ARETHUSA reported (0017/17) that 14 ships were sailing from Le Verdon for Falmouth p.m. 17th with about 1200 British refugees and also Madure *(MADURA?)* with 180 embassy Staff and 8000 refugees for the Bristol Channel.

S.N.O. St. Nazaire reported ((0119/17) that DUCHESS OF YORK with 4300 personnel, GEORGIC with 3982 were sailing for Plymouth, subsequently diverted to Liverpool, BATORY with 2000 for Plymouth & SOBEISKI with 2890 for Falmouth escorted by WHIRLWIND and BEAGLE.

LADY OF MANN arrived Plymouth from Brest 0450; CANTERBURY & MANXMAID AT 0521.

FRANCONIA was temporarily out of action due to near miss by bombs on the 16th, mainshaft and gearing out of line. At 0700/17th she proceeded independently from Quiberon Bay to Plymouth.

WESTCOTT arrived Brest   0540/17

BACTRIA arrived Plymouth   0715/17

VIENNA   "   "   0745/17

WOLVERINE having reported (0618/17) that a convoy of 19 loaded ships would be ready by noon, was instructed (0830/17) to escort them, taking with him trawlers AGATE & CAMBRIDGESHIRE C-in C W.A. ordered WESTCOTT (0834/17) to direct all ships, due for Brest into the harbour.

BRITANNY, TREWAL, TRELAWNY and CITY OF EVANSVILLE sailed Avomouth (0900/17) for Loire via Quiberon Bay.

STRATHAIRD and ORMONDE arrived Brest 1035/17 and at 1100/17 Brest reported that sufficient ships had arrived. WREN was instructed (1129/17) to join D.9.at St. Nazaire. At 1145/17 B.N.L.O. asked for transport for 3000 troops and 250 rearguard at La Pallice by noon 18th

The French ship CHAMPLAIN (28000 tons gross) was reported mined off La Pallice a.m. 17th but it was not believed that the port was blocked.

WOLVERINE reported (1245/17) that the convoy of 19 ships previously reported had grown to 26 ships including an oiler and had sailed from Quiberon bay for Bristol Channel at 4 knots.

PORT MONTREAL sailed Falmouth 1145/17 for Loire.

N.O.I/C. Avonmouth reported (1330/17) that BRITANNY would be delayed until daylight 18/6 through engine defects.

S.N.O. St. Nazaire reported (1445/17) that HAVELOCK had one engine out of action and was returning with LANCASTRIA to U.K. He asked for more destroyers as embarkation was badly delayed by lack of shipping.

PRINSES JOSEPHINE CHARLOTTE sailed Falmouth 1628/17 for Brest. PRINCESS MAUDE sailed 1600/17 with 2600 troops.

HIGHLANDER signalled (1603/17) that LANCASTRIA was hit and sinking. At 1843/17 D.9. reported that LANCASTRIA had been sunk by a bomb after loading. It was impossible to assess casualties. Survivors has *(sic)* been sailed in ORONSAY. D.9. reported that he only had HIGHLANDER and one with him and that embarkation would be seriously delayed. WREN & ZAZA were ordered (1822/17) to join him.

S.N.O. Brest reported 1507/17 that WESTCOTT had been holed by collision and was returning Plymouth at 8 knots. He asked for more destroyers immediately if possible.

KONINGIN EMMA arrived Plymouth (1838/17).

At 1851/17, C. in C. W.A. informed S.N.O. Brest, S.N.O. St. Nazaire and all ships in W.A. of the decision to withdraw the whole of the B.E.F. immediately and detailed the vessels that would be arriving at the various ports MACKAY was informed that they were to be embarked on any ship for the U.K.

ORMONDE, OTRANTO and ARANDORA STAR sailed Quiberon Bay p.m. /17 with orders to report to WOLVERINE.

S.N.O. Brest reported the situation at 1930/17 as total number embarked 30,000. All big ships sailing independently, MACKAY and trawler taking off small number remaining.

MACKAY was asked (2154/17) to confirm the authenticity of this message and did so (2307/17).

Senior British Army Officer, St. Nazaire was informed (1935/17) by War Office that certain troops would endeavour to destroy all British and French oil stocks in area St. Nazaire, Donges and Nantes before embarking.

STURDY was instructed (2011/17) to join MACKAY at Brest.

S.N.O. Brest reported (2027/17) that he had ordered WINCHESLEA to join D.9.at St. Nazaire and that no further destroyers were required at Brest.

MACKAY was ordered (2036/17) to send to La Pallice forthwith, ships with total capacity of 7000, including ETTRICK if possible. ARANDORA STAR was ordered (2137/17) to proceed forthwith to La Pallice, but reported (2217/17) that the signal had been received too late as all ships had sailed from Brest and ETTRICK had not been seen.

BATORY & WHIRLWIND arrived Plymouth (2145/17)

S.N.O. Brest, in MACKAY, signalled (2223/17) reference C. in C., W. A. that he had no information about any Belgians before leaving Brest at 2130.

WREN (2340/17) & AMSTERDAM (2351/17) sailed from Plymouth.

At 2342/17, S.N.O. St. Nazaire was requested to confirm statement of the French that embarkation in Loire would be completed during the night of 17th, and also whether this would include personnel, stores and M.T.

Commodore in JOHN HOLT reported 2343/17 that he was returning with 829 survivors from LANCASTRIA, many without clothing.

P.S.T.O. Southampton was instructed 2351/17 to sail ST. HELIER forthwith to La Pallice.

June 18th

ETTRICK & ORMONDE ordered to St. Nazaire (0003/18)

CLAN FERGUSON to Bordeaux (0004)

S.N.O. Brest reported (0031) that after several reversals of policy during Monday forenoon G.H.Q. had given instructions for personnel only to be loaded, about 25 guns had been loaded.

SOBEISKI arrived Falmouth (0100).D.9. reported (0100) that French statement to the effect that embarkation would be completed that night were utterly wrong.

CUTTY SARK sailed from Plymouth (0115)

ARANDORA STAR ordered to Quiberon Bay (0213)

WREN escorting AMSTERDAM & LADY OF MANN sailed for Plymouth (0224)

ORMONDE diverted from St. Nazaire to La Pallice (0238)

WHIRLWIND sailed for Gironde (0300)

S.N.O. Brest reported (0317) that French troops landed Brest Monday *(17th)* ex ROYAL SCOTSMAN from Narvik did not wish to be evacuated to the United Kingdom, 400 Polish in ULSTER MONARCH were allowed to remain in ship.

Brest reported mined. M/S COURTIER & ERIMO ordered to return there (0511)

STRATHAIRD arrived Plymouth (0608) MACKAY & ROYAL SCOTSMAN arrived Plymouth (0635). MACKAY brought back 49 Naval and Military Officers and 39 ratings and other ranks.

Convoy OLIVE sailed Loire (0630)	ROYAL ULSTERMAN	2800
	ULSTER PRINCE	2800
	FLORISTAN	2000

BAHARISTAN	2000
CLAN MACPHERSON *Ferguson?*	2000
DUNDRUM CASTLE	2000
DAVID LIVINGSTONE	2000
FABIAN	2000
CITY OF MOBILE	2000
GLEN AFFARIC *Glenaffric?*	4000

Escorted by VANOC & BEAGLE. Destination Plymouth & Falmouth.

D.9.ordered WINCHESLEA (0647) to send any small transports at Quiberon to St. Nazaire forthwith, and also ordered ROYAL ULSTERMAN back to St. Nazaire (0653). Brest and La Pallice closed, mines probable (0714)

S.N.O. St. Nazaire reported (0730) embarkation of personnel would be completed pm. Tuesday 18th, but no stores or M.T. for which no shipping was available.

BELLEROPHON arrived Plymouth (0745)

D9 ordered WINCHESLEA to St. Nazaire with all despatch (0805)

BEAGLE reported (0830) sailed from St. Nazaire for Plymouth (0600) with ULSTER PRINCE, CLAN FERGUSON, BAHARISTAN, each carrying approximately 3000 troops, DAVID LIVINGSTONE with 800, BEAGLE 600, all short of provisions. *(part OLIVE, contradicts 0630)*

At 0800 BROKE from British Naval Liaison Officer situation at 0800 18th June.

(1)   Detachment of stragglers being embarked in *(Prinses)* JOSEPHINE CHARLOTTE
(2)   Channel being swept after previous night's minelaying to enable French Fleet to leave
(3)   French Naval Authorities shewing no sign of individual initiative.
(4)   Enemy mechanical forces 150 miles away
(5)   All British motor transport abandoned.

CUTTY SARK stopped by mines off St. Mathieu (0845)

ACHERON reported (0845) meeting LYCAON with 800 troops on board and no rations in position 51. 00. N. 06. 00. W. proceeding Bristol Channel.

Trawler SUTHERNESS arrived Falmouth (0850)

ARETHUSA reported (0903) sailings from Le Verdun:-

Falmouth for orders, LAPWING, CANFORD CHINE, CRANE, ACAVUS, WINDSORWOOD, BARON JEDBURGH, TREVETHOE, AINDERBY, JENA, POMELIA, YARRAVILLE, GRONINGEN. Norwegian ships VARANG, FJELL, TARANGER, RUTENFJELL

To Dakar in convoy French ships VILLE DE HAVRE, MAGUERITIE FINALY, BOURGOGNE, GROIX, MARIS STELLA, TADORNE, PIERRE CLAUDE, MAURICE DELMAS, CARIMARE

FOXGLOVE instructed by Commander-in Chief, Portsmouth to endeavour to evacuate 10 tons of Suez Canal archives from Granville (0932)

HAVELOCK reported starboard propellor and tail shaft damaged, port propellor probably damaged

WESTCOTT in collision with s.s. NYROCA, holed in No 3 fuel tank,

D.9.signalled WOLVERINE (1054), transports urgently needed at Gironde

D.9. reported (1039) that VANOC had been placed at the disposal of General Brooke and staff, but that he had embarked on trawler (CAMBRIDGESHIRE)

Commander-in-Chief, Portsmouth, ordered SABRE & FERNIE (1107) to close Cherbourg to evacuate 800 troops and 50 Naval demolition ports? and to provide covering fire if required

Four aircraft bombing Brest (1153)

MACKAY ordered (1009) to proceed to Quiberon Bay by 0400/19, report and proceed thence to La Pallice under orders of D.9.

CUTTY SARK reported (1245) bombed, can only proceed slowly

COURTIER reported (1316) Brest and shipping being heavily bombed, shipping leaving S.N.O. St Nazaire reported all personnel evacuated St. Nazaire (1315/18)

BROKE reported (1346) statement from Belgian General that 4000 Belgian troops were 25 miles North and 2000 South of St. Nazaire. He had told them to make for St. Nazaire and was sending there JOSEPHINE CHARLOTTE & FERMAIN.

LYCAON arrived Milford Haven with troops (1436).

S.N.O. St. Nazaire reported (1440) all M.T. and store ships crammed to capacity with personnel. All holds in use and men short of food and water.

ARETHUSA reported (1444) requisitioning Dutch ship BENNEKON *(M)* to carry 400 refugees.

GUIDO arrived Plymouth 1452. BEAGLE directed to divert ULSTER PRINCE & DAVID LIVINGSTONE to Falmouth (1502)

D.9. reported that ARANDORA STAR was not required and was being sent to United Kingdom (1520)

S.N.O. St. Nazaire and D.9. informed (1526) that Commodore Hallet and party were arriving with special duties. Troops were being sent for his use but he might require others

ARETHUSA reported (1537) that no German prisoners were expected Bordeaux

ORANSAY (sic) with wounded and other survivors from "LANCASTRIA" and troops arrived Plymouth 1547

BROKE reported 1556 that French naval force was leaving Brest evening 18th, and that demolition was planned or midnight. This report crossed Commander-in Chief's 1602 stressing the importance of sailing or destruction of RICHELIEU & JEAN BART.

ST. HELIER was ordered to La Pallice and D.S.T.O. Plymouth was ordered to send MANXMAID & CANTERBURY to Brest, but ST HELIER arrived Plymouth 1700

At 1625 Commander-in-Chief directed S.N.O. St. Nazaire to keep fighters as long as possible in view of 6000 Belgians and unknown number of refugees still awaiting evacuation

ARANDORA STAR chased by, but escaped from U-boat

Admiral Ouest reported that Training Battleship PARIS was damaged by bomb and proceeding Plymouth escorted by GROENLAND & HEUREUX, also OURAGAN escorted by POMEROL. Admiral Ouest was sailing in LE HARDI for Casablanca or Dakar.

D.9. reported (1752) St. Nazaire evacuated and presumed in enemy hands. s.s. ETTRICK told not to proceed there

VANOC reported (1746) 8000 troops, am proceeding Plymouth

BROKE signalled that RICHELIEU had sailed with Admiral Ouest.

ORCADES arrived Plymouth 1803.

S.N.O. St. Nazaire reported (1817) having evacuated port at port 1315 with Brigadier Gill and staff.

CITY OF EVANSVILLE sailed Penzance 1800 for St. Nazaire

D.9. Reported :- (1828) Convoy: ROYAL ULSTERMAN, CITY OF LANCASTER, BELTOY, MAURICE ROSE, GLANLEA *(GLENLEA?)*, HARPATHIAN, GLENDENNING, POLLUX, LECHISTAN containing troops sailed 1100

Also in company British Military Hospital Ship ROBERT E. HOLT, oiler CASPIA, Polish LEWANT, Trawlers ST. MELANTE & CLOUGHTON WYKE, OSAMA, ARMENA escorted HIGHLANDER & WREN.

Trawler LACERTO arrived Plymouth, 1910. ORONSAY 1547.

Commander-in Chief enquired (1943) whether ARETHUSA had sufficient tonnage for evacuation of GIRONDE. ARETHUSA informed that most important that special service agents at Arcachon, ordered by Admiralty to proceed to Bordeaux or Le Verdun, be got away. ARETHUSA told to try and contact General of fully equipped Czech division comprising 1200 men, including aircraft, and inform him transport to United Kingdom will be provided if he can get forces to Bordeaux before enemy interference with route.

D.9. was told (2006) to proceed to La Pallice, when satisfied nothing more could be done at Loire and to divert shipping to La Pallice – trawlers and A/S Yachts would be at her disposal   At 2054 MACKAY was too ordered to proceed to La Pallice.

Customs Jersey signalled that the Master of s.s. HODDER reported on arrival that he had sighted enemy seaplane dropping magnetic mines in harbour at 0230.

MAID MARION reported (2100) that French Authorities stated St. Nazaire in enemy hands. STURDY was ordered to proceed to Plymouth at 2041.

MACKAY reported (2215) French Battleship COURBET off Ushant steering North.

VANQUISHER reported (1600) having seen French Admiral who hoped to sail Battleship 0500/19 – arrangements made to destroy if unable to sail. *(Courbet?)*

Admiralty informed (1711) BERKLEY, General Julius Deutsch and wife onboard s.s. Cuba at Bordeaux, permitted to proceed to United Kingdom in any merchant vessel.

CUTTY SARK reported starboard engine out of action, returning Plymouth at 8 knots.

BROKE reported 1815 that French A.M.C.s EXPLORATEUR & GRANDIDIER had been ordered to St. Ives Bay by Admiral Ouest.

During the day Trawlers MONTANO, OSWALDIAN, & LADY ESTELLE and tugs TANGA & PERSIA arrived Falmouth.

Commander-in-Chief ordered 1914 VIENNA, ST. JULIAN, ST. ANDREW, CYCLOPS & BELLEROPHON to Dartmouth, PRINCE ALBERT to Southampton and BACTRIA to Barry.

ARETHUSA ordered (1925) WHIRLWIND to intercept and escort MADURA out from Le Verdun to Falmouth and NARIVA to B.C. both carrying refugees.

C. in C ordered Falmouth to sail GUINNEAN *(GUINEAN)* to Barry

CAMBRIDGESHIRE reported E.T.A. Plymouth 1500/19 with British general Staff on board

s.s. JOHN HOLT arrived Plymouth 2025, CIMBULA *(CYMBULA)* 2100

At 2058 LORD GREY & BERVIE BRAES were ordered to La Pallice, ST.MALANTE, ASAMO, OVETAS to Gironde.

ARETHUSA signalled (2114) she had enough tonnage for known refugees. Belgian KASONGO had been requisitioned for evacuating special service agents.

VIVA II, referring to MAID MARION's 2100, reported St. Nazaire not in enemy hands, but no British troops there.

At 2309 H. Ship ST. JULIAN arrived Plymouth, KONINGEN EMMA sailed 2244.

June 19th

KINDAT diverted to Barry (0011)

ORACLE signalled (0012/19) that the Germans were close to St. Nazaire at 2330/18. ORACLE returning with rescued merchant crews, a few soldiers and refugees, 250 in all. *(see 1800/19)*

Rescue tugs SALVONIA ZWARTEZEE and MARAUDER ordered to return to Falmouth (0014).

French A.M.C. EXPLORATEUR GRANDIDIER *(one ship, previous entry 1815 suggests two?)* diverted from St. Ives to Milford (0016)

German aircraft reported ARETHUSA possibly laying magnetic mines Le Verdon (0028)

Admiralty informed ARETHUSA & BERKLEY (0035/19) that French Colonel Bonevita was proceeding by air to Bordeaux to arrange evacuation of individual French Officers and men, and skilled workmen who wished to leave France. C in C. W.A. was asked to arrange transport, preferably in French ships, for 2000 to start with.

Trawler FLORA, motor barge CABBY arrived Plymouth (0045)

ARETHUSA reported two more bombing attacks Le Verdon between 0130 and 0150.

ORMONDE ordered to La Pallice, Gironde area (0216)

PORT MONTREAL to Barry (0219)

B.N.L.O. Bordeaux requested (0330/19) for shipping suitable for entry Bayonne harbour to collect about 1000 refugees. Hospital ships, ST. ANDREW, ST. JULIEN left Plymouth (0450)

ISLESMAN, BOVEY TRACEY, CORBRIDGE, HAMPSHIRE COAST arrived Plymouth (0520)

Trawler MURMANSK grounded at Brest and abandoned (0542) – crew saved.

JOZO, BARON LOVAT, CAPULET, arrived Plymouth (0610)

ARETHUSA reported (0548) sailing of refugee ships from Le Verdon, MADURA for Falmouth and NARIVA for the Bristol Channel.

IMOGEN & GRIFFIN ordered (0551) to take over tow of French destroyer OURAGAN in position 57.N. 05. 03. W.

Hospital Ship DORSETSHIRE arrived Plymouth (0652)

Tug QUEENSCROSS reported (0700) that she was off Brest but refused permission to enter.

s.s. GLENAFFARIC arrived Plymouth (0751)

French tugs ATTENTIF, CHAMPION and Belgian Pilot Vessel BATEAU arrived Plymouth with refugees from St. Malo.

C. in C. W.A. (0825) instructed local establishments to prepare to receive French and Belgian Naval Officers and ratings.

BROKE reported (0834) that she had left Brest 0030. Demolition largely effective. All French warships out of harbour except two submarines scuttled. Evacuation of French troops still in progress. Now leaving BERTHEAUME for Plymouth with 20 British stragglers, 20 civilians (12 women), and 180 Polish troops.

LORD GREY reported (0845) that on arrival off St. Nazaire she intercepted a signal stating that it was in German hands. She was returning with trawler BERVIE BRAES.

L/L Trawlers LA ROCHELLE & INVERFORTH arrived La Verdon (0915)

VANQUISHER reported (0915) French Battleship JEAN BART and two French destroyers with Admiral Ouest in LE HARDI had sailed for Casablanca.

WREN reported (0950) in company with THISTLEGLEN & PHILLIPPA *(PHILLIP M?)* carrying 2500 troops for Falmouth.

French despatch vessel SUIPPE arrived Falmouth (0950)

CLAN FERGUSON & BAHARISTAN arrived Plymouth

French s.s. MEKNES arrived from Brest with approximately 3000 French troops, 11 civilians, 1 French Admiral and 1 French General.

TRELAWNY reported St. Nazaire roads attacked (1007)

Liverpool ordered to sail (1129) M.T. GEORGIC forthwith to La Pallice.

Sea Transport staff from St. Nazaire and Quiberon Bay arrived Plymouth (1016)

Tug KROOMAN ordered by D.9. (1017) to proceed to La Pallice.

BROKE (1025) intercepted French S/Ms MINERVE & JUNON in tow of QUEENS CROSS & WATERCOCK off Pierres Noires escorted by PESSAC and SAUTESNE and proposed escorting to Plymouth. Ordered tug STURDY to tow JUNON, tug being short of coal.

B.N.L.O. France reported (1026) unable to contact Czech General – re-evacuating Czech troops. D.9 reported (1035) convoy Stable 2 with 1200 troops in position 47. 52. N. 06. 21. W. course 000° 8 knots.

MACKAY (1041) stated La Pallice gate shut, ALDERPOOL & LADY OF MANN outside. Endeavouring to get it opened.

ULSTER MONARCH ordered from Falmouth to La Pallice (1136).

VISCOUNT, WITCH arrived Plymouth (1152).

TWICKENHAM FERRY arrived Plymouth (1251).

Admiralty (1271) advised C. in C. W.A. ARETHUISA & BERKELEY

re Polish troops 25000 in Ports between Brest, Vannes & Rochelle, 5000 between Bordeaux & Bayonne.

3000 now, but may reach Marseilles or Bordeaux and said every effort should be made to bring them to the U.K.

PUNJABI & HARVESTER joined convoy Stable 2 (1226).

CUTTY SARK arrived Plymouth (1236).

m.v. SWAY arrived Plymouth (1236).

French Transport PLM 17 arrived (1330).

MACKAY reported (1321) situation La Pallice. MAID MARION in company. British S.N.O. left with last British troops. None further expected. 10 refugees embarked MAID MARION. A few Polish soldiers sighted.

TRELAWNEY heavily bombed St. Nazaire Roads, damage slight (1325)

WREN ordered (1347) to take ships to Newport (THISTLEGLEN & PHILLIPPA – routed for Falmouth)

VANOC (1412) reported loading of British ships.

CITY OF MOBLIE	3000 troops with		5 stretcher cases
FLORISTAN	3500		
ESSEX DRUID	1500	"	5 stretcher cases
DUNDRUM CASTLE	500		

FLORISTAN damaged in engine room by bombing.

French battleship PARIS arrived Plymouth (1425)

ARETHUSA reported (1457) several magnetic mines laid during night. One French merchant vessel sunk a.m. 19th. One mine believed exploded prematurely. 2, possibly 3 aircraft destroyed

Using L/L trawlers to sweep passage for ARETHUSA & BERKLEY. Embassy ordered ARETHUSA to sail for U.K. as soon as British staff embarked p.m.

French s.s. POULMIC, Cable Vessel EMILE BAUNER, escort vessels CHALUPIER, HEUREUX, & ROLAND, British s.s. HYTHE arrived (1500) Plymouth.

D.9.(1519) reported that he was rejoining convoy Stable 2. Troops without food and water.

French tug ABEILLE 8 arrived Plymouth

IMOGEN, PUNJABI, GRIFFIN, WITCH, HARVESTER, VISCOUNT ordered to St. Nazaire (1534) also transports ROYAL SCOTSMAN & SOBEISKI.

Refugee ships sailed Le Verdon for Falmouth (1546):- STAD HARLEM & ALCOR with 150 each, BENNEKOM with 400, RONBUR III (ROBUR III) & REGNSTROOM (REGGESTROOM) with unknown numbers

Tug MAUR*** arrived Falmouth (1550)

MANOR reported (1555) she had on board 67 Naval Ratings, 2 Army Officers and 25 O.R. and 1 civilian. CHILTERN had 114 evacuees.

STURDY arrived Plymouth (1548), transports PRINCESS MAUD and TYNEWALL (TYNWALD)

(1600). French crane lighters GEORGES DE JOLLY & ANDRE BLONDEL arrived (1618)

TRELAWNEY ordered to Barry (1648)

B.N.L.O. Bordeaux informed (1649) ships to embark third Polish Division sent St. Nazaire, others to La Pallice.

Plymouth arrivals: Transports ROYAL SOVEREIGN, FLORISTAN, CITY OF MOBILE, FARRIAN, ST BRIAC , DUNDRUM CASTLE, French PRESTIN (1700 – 1720).

Sailings GALATEA & BEAGLE (1710).

Trawler CAMBRIDGESHIRE with General Brooke and staff arrived (1720)

D.9. ordered (1731) to divert to St Nazaire OTRANTO, ORONTES, ARANDORA STAR, ST. HELIER, ETTRICK.

ARETHUSA reported (1735) wreck of French ship MEXIQUE dangerous to navigation off Le Verdon.

WINCHESLEA instructed by C- in-C. W.A. (1752) that two to three thousand from Stable 2 were to be landed at Falmouth Ships to be diverted accordingly.

ORMONDE attacked by aircraft (1754) and (1808)

ORACLE reported (1800) her passengers consisted of 44 soldiers, 25 white merchant seamen,31 Chinese seamen, 12 European refugees, 1 Naval Officer, 1 military hospital case. Total 114 and not 250 as reported 0012/19.

BERKLEY instructed by Admy. (1823/19) that a most important and urgent message for Admiral Darlan would reach him shortly and he was to remain in Bordeaux until he had delivered the message and received a reply.

LL Trawler BERVIE BRAES reported (1830) I am leaking badly and have only one day's coal left

M/S Trawlers STRATHRANNOCK, WILLIAM BELL & SEDDON sailed Plymouth (1835)

MACKAY (1901) stated that he expected to ship 3000 Polish troops in ALDERPOOL 19th

VISCOUNT & WITCH sailed Plymouth (1905)

Arrivals at Dartmouth (1915) CANTERBURY, MANX MAID, SAINT ANDREW, ST. JULEIN, CYCLOPS, BELLEROPHON, RASK, SAMBRE, FLUEL, MARK 4, FLORA.

Arrived at Plymouth 1800 French Tugs ABEILLE 4 and AD 100, Trawler N.U, motor yacht TORBAY BELLE, s.s. CHARMA

ORMONDE reported air attack ceased (1920)

ARETHUSA informed (1930) essential Gironde and La Pallice be kept clear of mines. LL vessels to be retained, orders being sent.

Admiralty advised (1943) that ALERT should be sailed as soon as escort was available to cut Brest-Fayal and Brest-Cape Cod cables.

Arrived Plymouth (1950) M/S Trawlers COUTIER & ERMO, French Trawler A.D. 120 and INGINIER DE JOLY.

B.N.L.O. Bordeaux informed (1930) that evacuation of Polish government was of importance.

AMSTERDAM & MANXMAN arrived and sailed Plymouth (2015)

WHIRLWIND reported (2025) MADURA e.t.a. Falmouth 1030/20 with 1370 refugees. NARIVA 265 for Bristol Channel.

Admiralty asked (2053) to give early consideration to laying of magnetic mines in French ports immediately they are evacuated.

GEORGIC sailed Liverpool for La Pallice (2030)

D.9. instructed (2103) that SOBEISKI and destroyers were to evacuate 8000 Polish troops from St.Nazaire.

MACKAY advised (2104) that as no air protection was available ships evacuating were to remain underway as much as possible.

N.O.I/C Dartmouth instructed (2121) to divert AMSTERDAM & MANXMAN – due at 2245 – to Milford Haven.

ARETHUSA reported (2153) British Ambassador and 30 staff leaving for Arcachon. Majority of personnel sailing in ARETHUSA 19[th.] KONINGIN EMMA ordered to be available for evacuating refugees from fortress as ordered by British Consul. LL Trawlers sent to Arcachon.

BERKLEY proceeding Arcachon

P.S.T.O. Southampton instructed (2158) to sail BLAIRNEVIS, BLEGRAVIAN *(BELGRAVIAN)*

DELIUS, for La Pallice – Gironde area.

D.9. ordered (2239) to return to Plymouth in HIGHLANDER.

PUNJABI & ATHERSTONE ordered to Clyde on completion of present duties (2259)

C-in-C W.A. (2301) instructed GLEN HOLT camp, R.M.B., Impregnable, Raleigh, Gdynia, N.B. that all French, Polish, Belgian and other Nationals, service or civilian, landed from France were to be identified as early as possible.

s.s. MURRAYFIELD arrived Cawsand Bay (2315)

French destroyer OURAGEN arrived (2320)

Lorient reported all clear by S.N.O. (2321)

IMOGEN instructed to act as S.N.O. Loire during absence of D.9. (2322)

MACKAY reported (2345) enemy bombing La Pallice.

HIGHLANDER arrived Plymouth with D.9. and Captain Hamilton (2350)

French Naval vessels, 1 sloop, 1 patrol vessel, 1 gunboat, 4 armed trawlers, 1 M.T.B. arrived Falmouth 2350.

Captain of CYMBULA reported (2355) that he had on board 250 army ranks - short of kit - and two women survivors from LANCASTRIA.

June 20th

HARVESTER, IMOGEN, PUNJABI ordered to return to Plymouth (0026)

Belgian PRINCE BAUDOUIN arrived (0030)

N.O.I/C Dartmouth ordered to sail VIENNA, CANTERBURY & MANXMAN to Plymouth

Tug KROOMAN ordered (0104) to proceed to La Pallice replied (0115) "cannot ascertain position La Pallice have only general chart" ordered to return Falmouth (0336)

A/S Yacht ORACLE and French Tug IMOGEN arrived (0100)

STURDY ordered (0144) to proceed to Southampton with DUNDRUM CASTLE, MCKARES *(MEKNES?)*, CITY OF MOBILE.

French S/M SURCOUF arrived (0230)

C. in C. Portsmouth informed SABRE (0246) that 5000 Polish troops were reported fighting towards St. Malo SABRE to proceed St. Helier to standby to escort schoots to St. Malo.

STURDY sailed (0310) DUNDRUM CASTLE, MCKARES & CITY OF MOBILE (0445) with 6500 troops

ARETHUSA reported (0501) that enemy laid parachute mines and it was believed No. of St. George's Bank and main Channel near Falaise Bank buoy were mined.

WINCHELSEA & ROYAL SCOTSMAN with 300 troops detached from convoy to Falmouth at 0500 by VANQUISHER.

Trawlers MANOR, ROCHEBONNE, CHILTERN, CLOUGHTON WYKE & LORRAINE arrived Plymouth (05x5)

MACKAY reported (0600) sailed ALDERPOOL with 4000 Polish troops and EMPIRE INDUSTRY with 40 British refugees for Falmouth.

ZAZA arrived Gironde (0610)

BATORY ordered to Bayonne (0616)

HARVESTER arrived Plymouth (0620)

Tug WATERCOCK arrived Falmouth (0640)

OAKBANK & SKJOLD arrived Plymouth (0650) BERVIE BRAES (0720)

MANXMAN, VIENNA, CANTERBURY sailed (0700)

BERKLEY reported (0735) that last information from Embassy at (1700/19) indicated that situation should still be satisfactory at Biscarosse.

French Trawler P.46 and OPQA arrived Plymouth (0735)

French Yacht OTDB towing lifeboat and OPNE (0740) with four French tugs.

MACKAY reported (0814) SOBEISKE arrived Le Verdon and had been ordered to St. Helier

(? presumably to embark Polish troops from St. Malo)

Five French armed trawlers and eight French motor craft arrived Plymouth (0815)

SABRE reported (0830) shadowed by enemy A/C south of Casquets.

WINCHELSEA reported (0848) she had on board Captain Allen R.N. and eight Naval Officers one French lady secretary, Brigadier Gill and 7 army Officers: one merchant officer, one sick Polish W.O., 8 Naval Ratings, 10 military and one civil airman.

BERKLEY reported (0855) departure delayed owing to mining of channel E.T.A. Arcachon 1300 Tugs SALVONIA, QUEENSCROSS, WATERCOCK & ZWARTE ZEE (Dutch) arrived Falmouth (0910) BROKE & WINCHELSEA arrived Plymouth (0927), CANTERBURY (0928), MANXMAN (0950) & VIENNA (1015).

WHIRLWIND reported (0935) am escorting NARIVA to Milford Haven

B.N.L.O. Bordeaux informed Admiralty (0943) that Polish Division was assembling Le Verdon and requested shipping be re-directed there to report to French Marine.

BERKLEY reported (1005) French cruiser PRIMAUGUET anchored in position 45. 40. N. 01. 3.W (North of Gironde)

139

SABRE reported to C. in C. Portsmouth (1035) that she was escorting three transports with evacuees from St. Helier.

B.N.L.O. Bordeaux reported (1032) some members of Polish Government evacuated in ARETHUSA. Trying to instruct remainder to embark with Polish troops. Urgent requirements BAYONNE, transports for 1000 military personnel and refugees.

Garronne river handed over to French. Polish Authorities B.N.L.O. leaving Bordeaux.

ULSTER MONARCH ordered to La Pallice – Gironde area (1047) to return to U.K. if no British warships met in vicinity.

VANQUISHER reported (1050) having following on board:- Cdr. Halett, 3 officers and 40 ratings of demolition party. Capt. Schurr, D.S.T.O. Nantes and ? Norton R.N.V.R. 3 Polish Officers and 1 Polish Private, 5 Polish women with 4 children - families of Polish Officers.

IMOGEN reported PUNJABI sailed (1056) for Plymouth from St. Nazaire with 400 Polish troops (see also later signal (2157)) No more in St. Nazaire, or expected there.

IMOGEN, GRIFFIN, WITCH & VISCOUNT proceeded to RADE DE CROISIC where it was hoped to fill up all destroyers. ETTRICK & SOBEISKI not arrived St. Nazaire

SABRE reported (1112) to Portsmouth still about 15000 people in Jersey, and asked for all available small craft.

C. in C. Portsmouth informed SABRE (1110) St. Malo apparently still in French hands – and report - SABRE to ascertain if Polish troops still awaiting evacuation, if so embark them in 18 Dutch schoots then en route St. Helier.

French Tug AMOGAT towing two French S/M Chasers arrived Plymouth (1110), two French S/Ms (1120)

VANQUISHER arrived Plymouth (1140)

BEAGLE arrived Le Verdon (1000) and sailed for Bordeaux (1110)

ARETHUSA sailed Le Verdon (1120) for Plymouth bringing President of Poland and staff, British Ambassador to Poland and staff, Staff of British Embassies Brussels and Paris–250 in all.

D.9. re-embarked in HAVELOCK (1210)

GEORGIC ordered back to Liverpool (1210)

Falmouth instructed (1240) to sail ULSTER MONARCH to Plymouth. Sailed (1830)

Polish General Sikorski arrived Bordeaux pm/19/6

BERKLEY instructed (1300/20) to give him all assistance

French S/M chaser No. 11 arrived Plymouth (1311)

BERKLEY ordered Admiralty (1312) to get in touch with Feller & Co., 1, Espirit de Lois, Bordeaux, and arrange shipment of vital goods ex. Goth Co., Switzerland.

Arrived Plymouth (1225 – 1330) s.s. CASPIA, CITY OF LANCASTER, GLENDINNING, BRAMWELL, GLENLEA, HARPATION, ROBERT L. HOLT, BELTOY, PURBECK, COLLUX, LUVANT.

C.S.2. informed (1351) by C-in-C W.A. Polish division assembling Le Verdon for evacuation. Also 3000 French air pilots and mechanics. Shipping at La Pallice, LADY OF MANN, ORMONDE, KONINGIN EMMA, on passage thither St. Helier (ST. HELIER) PR INCESS BEATRIX, BLAIR NEVIS, DELIUS.

Trawler STRATHRANNOCK arrived Plymouth (1440)

Sailed from Le Verdon for Falmouth (1152)

> KASANGO with 100 British passengers
>
> NIGERSTROOM with 600 British passengers
>
> VILLE DE LEIGE with 200-300 Polish and Czech troops.
>
> BROOMPARK with unknown number British and machine tools

Mr. Campbell at Bordeaux reported (1229) to Foreign Office and C-in-C W.A. that 5000 Polish army were assembling at Le Verey and 10000 at La Rochelle.

Belle Isle bombed (1401)

IMOGEN reported (1425), Have sailed GRIFFIN+ for Plymouth with 350 Polish troops, am embarking a further 900 approximately in WITCH, VISCOUNT & IMOGEN. *(see Imogen 1730)* Polish authorities state no further troops in vicinity capable of being evacuated.

GRIFFIN reported (1448) have met ETTRICK off Belle Isle and told her to remain in company.

ROYAL SCOTSMAN also present.

La Pallice roads bombed (MACKAY 1620)

Lifeboat with 23 French refugees arrived St. Mary's Scilly (1635)

MACKAY signalled (1647) Can do no more at La Pallice, empty transports are merely targets for enemy aircraft and are short of water with no prospect of troops. French are proceeding with destruction of oil storages. Am returning with ST. HELIER, LADY OF MANN in company. (sailed 1915).

CYCLOPS ordered (1711) to sail Dartmouth to La Pallice – Gironde forthwith, returning U.K. if no British warship in vicinity.

IMOGEN, reference his (1425), reported (1730) numbers evacuated WITCH 340, VISCOUNT 500, IMOGEN 466 including 3 British and 14 Belgian soldiers.

C.S.2 informed (1750) by C-in-C W.A. of report (1229) from Bordeaux also activities Col. Bonavita of French Army at Bordeaux.

BEAGLE instructed (1702) if demolitions completed he should proceed to La Pallice and carry out similar operation.

Admiralty signalled GALETEA (1755) to request French General Massenet Marancount to fly aircraft from CASAUX and MERIIGNAC aerodrome to Andover.

Arrivals Plymouth	French s.s. MOUSSE-LE-MOY	(1738)
	Tug FRENE	(1725)
	Tug CHERBOURGEORN No 4	(1730)
	Trawler B 1031	(1728)
	Aux. M/Y NIVERNAIS	(1757)

GRIFFIN instructed (1808) to send ETTRICK and ROYAL SCOTSMAN to La Pallice – Gironde area to report to any British warship.

P.L.M. 16 reported (1813) attacked by aircraft (1835) "All right"

BEAGLE instructed (1855) to endeavour to get in touch with B.N.L.O. Bordeaux and evacuate anyone he requires.

GRIFFIN reported (1902) VISCOUNT detailed to escort BRITANNY past Ushant. GRIFFIN and WITCH escorting KAIPAKI *(?)*, ROYAL SCOTSMAN. French destroyer MISTRAL arrived Plymouth (1900), bringing Vice Admiral CAYOL.

GRIFFIN asked (1945) reference C-in-C W.A. 1808, if ships should be sent to La Pallice in view of MACKAY's 1647

ULSTER MONARCH arrived (1930) Plymouth

French trawler MONIQUE-ANDREE towing launch (1954)

WHIRLWIND escorting NARIVA arrived Milford (2002)

Admiralty informed C-in-C W.A. (2013) of personnel it was desired to withdraw from France.

1. (a) La Rochelle area Up to 10000 Poles (reported) and up to 5000 Belgians – possibly.

   (b) Bordeaux area. Polish Division assembling 3000 French air pilots and mechanics   Possibly 5000 Czechs

   [c] Bayonne area. Some of the above proceeded to Bayonne

2. In addition number of French troops expected to respond to General' De Gaulle's appeal 3 or 4 ships to proceed Bayonne to convey these to Nt. Africa.

3. Most valuable store and equipment at Bordeaux should be lifted. (C-in-C's reply 2304)

Trawler ARSENAL reported (2055) having met Belgian s.s. PERSIER with 51 British Officers on board bound for Barry Roads.

PUNJABI reported (2157) have on board 365 Poles, 30 British soldiers and 14 others, including 18 wounded, mostly stretcher cases.

MACKAY instructed (2211) to send ST. HELIER and LADY OF MANN to Le Verdon for water and to embark any troops there.

ROYAL SCOTSMAN ordered to join MACKAY off Gironde entrance and ETTRICK to proceed Bayonne (2211)

C. in C. informed Admiralty (2304) with reference to Admiralty's 2031 that additional ships were being sent as follows:-

To Gironde	ORMONDE	Personnel	5000	due now
and	BATORY	"	3000	at present ordered Bayonne

Cargo ships BLAIRNEVIS, BELGRAVIAN, DELIUS, GLENAFFRIC, CYCLOPS, BECKENHAM, CLAN FERGUSON, LYCAON, MAPLEWOOD, CLAN ROSS, BALFE, CLAUMET *(CALUMET)*, KELSO, KUFRA, BARON KENNARD *(KINNARD?)*, KERMA, BARON NAIRN, all suitable for stores and two to three thousand personnel each, all due evening 21st and after.

To Bayonne	SOBEISKI	Personnel	3000	there now
	ETTRICK	"	3000	due pm 21st
	ARANDORA STAR	"	6000	due early 23rd

These ships will be in danger from air attack. Can French fighters assist?

s.s. BACPORT arrived Plymouth 2300 and H.M.S. STURDY 2320.

H.M. Trawler ONETOS with French Yacht in tow 2355

June 21st

WREN arrived Milford Haven 0015

Reference C. in C. W.A's 2211/20 MACKAY reported (0029) that both ETTRICK & ROYAL SCOTSMAN stated that they had only sufficient fuel to reach U.K. MACKAY therefore escorting both to Plymouth.

GRIFFIN & WITCH arrived Plymouth 0817

D.S.T.O. Barry ordered (0336) to sail the following ships for Gironde: BARON KINNARD, BARON NAIRN, KERMA.

D.S.T.O. Swansea ordered (0337) to sail KELSO, KUFRA, & LYCAON for Gironde.

D.S.T.O. Avonmouth ordered (0338) to sail CALUMET, for Gironde.

P.S.T.O. Southampton ordered (0339) to sail CLAN ROSS, MAPLEWOOD, BALFE & KYNO for Gironde.

D.S.T.O. Plymouth ordered (0341) to sail CLAN FERGUSON for Gironde

D.S.T.O. Falmouth ordered (0342) to sail BEKENHAM for Gironde

BERKLEY ordered by C.S.2. (0430) to proceed Le Verdon with all despatch and order any transports available to embark troops, sailing them as loaded for Plymouth.

Arrived Plymouth 0540:- NEPHRITE, MALPRIX, YEW PARK, MARSWORTH,

Arrived Plymouth 0552 French destroyer CDT. DUBOC

Arrived Plymouth 0640 SKEENA, ST. LAURENT, FRASER, RESTIGOUCHE.

Arrived Plymouth 0633 PUNJABI

Arrived Plymouth 0645 REVENGE, and at 0700 Tug KROOMAN

Arrived Plymouth 0801 ARETHUSA with Polish President M. Raczkiewicz and his wife with staff and other passengers (See also in message 1120/20)

WARLABY sailed Dartmouth (0730)

VIVA II reported (0930) ship with secret call sign 2 INV reports La Pallice in enemy hands.

BEAGLE informed by C. in C. W.A. (1014) that Commander Hallettt was sailing VANQUISHER at (1000) for La Pallice to assist in carrying out the duty.

ARANDORA STAR arrived Plymouth (1027), IMOGEN (1038)

BROOMPARK arrived Falmouth from Bordeaux (0600)

VISCOUNT reported (1045) many Polish soldiers were evacuated in civilian clothes preparatory to escaping to Spain. Rigorous scouting recommended.

VANQUISHER sailed Plymouth (1050) and H.M.T. LOMBARD arrived.

B.N.L.O. Bordeaux reported (1054) about 200 refugees being evacuated from Bayonne tonight. Shipping required for 3000 more.

VISCOUNT arrived Plymouth 1115

French Trawler 3402 arrived (1007)

PHILANTE informed C. in C. Portsmouth (1132) he had embarked GOVERNOR of Jersey with wife and A.D.C.

B.N.L.O. Bordeaux reported (1206) about 6000 Polish troops assembling at Le Verdon. No ship arrived yet.

C. in C. W.A. instructed C.S.2 (1218) to sail Falmouth in convoy or groups Belgian and Dutch troops to Avonmouth. Other nationalities Liverpool (except those for North Africa). Civilians to Falmouth.

MAID MARION ordered (1228) to escort ALDERPOOL to Liverpool and send EMPIRE ABILITY to Falmouth.

CALUMET sailed Avonmouth 1304

C. in C. Portsmouth requested (1314) to sail CALCUTTA to join C.S.2 as soon as read.

m.v. P. RAPOULT arrived Plymouth (1151), PRINCESS BEATRIX (1344)

STRATHAIRD in Sound, instructed (1403) to prepare to receive one thousand additional French sailors from merchant ships PENCHATEAU & GRAVELINNES.

Party "Z" ordered to be on board FRASER by 1630/21

BERKLEY reported 1515 Captain of port not helpful. Troops in wood behind Le Verdon.

B.N.L.O. (1521) stated he was arranging parties now at Arcachon, including ladies, to be embarked before nightfall.

French Trawler FARAULT arrived Plymouth from Brest (1530) with 3 children, 5 Naval Officer, 34 ratings, 4 Army Officers, 51 other ranks, 11 civilians all French 2 civilians - Spanish Naval Officers

French PENCHATEAU arrived Plymouth (1553)

French destroyer LE TRIOMPHANT (1643) arrived Plymouth.

MACKAY reported (1616) LADY OF MANN has one member of civilian crew seriously wounded, and has 11 refugees on board.

French GRAVELINNES arrived Plymouth (1663)

(17--) arrived Cawsand Bay ARZENITH, A.D. 376, BLACIDAI, FAROULT, POURQUOI PAS, the later with three British soldiers.

Trawler GEORGETTE reported (1700) returning to Plymouth as unable to contact BEAGLE.

MACKAY arrived Plymouth (1700)

Arrived (1705) French naval pinnace manned by eight ratings and French trawler RENE MARIE with seven crew, two French refugee seamen, six French army officers and two N.C.Os

LADY OF MANN & ST. HELIER arrived (1710) Plymouth. 9 passengers in LADY OF MANN, some wounded.

Arrived Plymouth (1752) French destroyer BOUCLIER and Tug MAMMOUT.

French S/M CHASER II sailed (1755)

BERKLEY stated Franco-Polish Liaison Officer reported 8000 Polish troops now here (Bordeaux) more arriving.

GEORGETTE & LORD GREY were ordered (1840) to proceed to St. Jean de Luz, if they had sufficient fuel and were able to Sweep, and to take their orders from GALETEA on arrival.

Orders were given (1858) for ARANDORA STAR to proceed to Bayonne under orders of an escort at 2150. Further orders would be signalled to her on arrival on arrival by a warship in the vicinity of the coast.

F.O.I/C Liverpool was informed (1859) that ALDERPOOL with 4000 Polish troops on board, escorted by MAID MARION, would arrive at 0130/23.   MANX MAID, PRINCESS MAUD & AMSTERDAM arrived at Milford Haven 1900.

MAID MARION signalled that she proposed to proceed to Falmouth with ALDERPOOL as there was no food left for the 4000 Polish troops.

GALATEA was informed (1902) that Captain Allen in H.M.C.S FRASER with beach and communication parties would sail for St. Jean de Luz, which would be used for evacuation in preference to Bayonne. VANQUISHER & BEAGLE were to be used as required by C.S.2

RESTIGOUCHE was ordered (1904) to escort ARANDORA STAR to Bayonne and place herself under the orders of C.S.2.

BERKLEY reported (1910) that no transport had arrived at Bordeaux. The entrance to the port was closed at night, and a small French merchant ship had exploded a magnetic mine 105° Pointe de Grave 1.3 at 1632. Little damage had been done.

BERKLEY was still not in touch with the Embassy.

Orders were given (1958) for VIENNA to sail to Southampton, TYNWALD & MANXMAN to Liverpool.

C.S.2 was ordered (2002) to endeavour to arrange with the Feller Company to ship all Oerlicken guns and other important material in Bordeaux.

MAID MARION was ordered (2029) to bring ALDERPOOL to Plymouth.

LORD GREY requested (2040) that instructions should be sent to ROYAL SCOTSMAN; who was awaiting MACKAY at Gironde, and enquired the position of GLENAFFRIC.

SABRE reported (2046) that only about 8000 people wished to be evacuated from Jersey. These had been embarked. Half the population of St. Peter Port, Guernsey, were willing to be evacuated and were being embarked. A French fishing vessel bringing 25 French subjects including 3 women and 3 children from Brittany to St. Helier had been intercepted, and the passengers transferred to the schoot DESPATCH.

BEAGLE reported (2121) 12 magnetic mines had been dropped between Le Verdon and PAULLAC, and asked for sweepers to cover this area on the morning flood tide.

The Captain of the French ship GRAVELINNES asked for food for 500 people on board. (2130)

MAID MARION reported (2145) that she expected to arrive at Plymouth 0330/22 and asked that provisions and water be supplied for ALDERPOOL as soon as possible.

GALATEA signalled (2152) that she was making every effort to get the stores away from Bordeaux and she was asked (2155) to ascertain whether any Polish or Belgian troops required to be embarked in the vicinity of La Pallice. If so she was to have them embarked in any ships available and escort them in convoy to Plymouth, with any other Allied ships she could take, keeping well clear of the French coast.

C. in C. W.A. reported (2223) that demands for fuel and other stores were being received from French ships at Plymouth, and asked whether these demands should be met.

MACKAY was asked (2229) what her last instructions to ORMONDE were, and she replied (2254) that she had ordered ORMONDE at 0800/22 to remain at sea in the vicinity of La Pallice until she received further instructions.

C.S.2 was informed (2258) that the following ships had been ordered to Gironde and to report on arrival to any British warship, DELIUS, GLENAFFRIC, CLAN FERGUSON, BLAIRNEVIS, CYCLOPS, BECKENHAM, CLAN ROSS, BALFE, KYNO, KUFFRA, KELSO, MAPLEWOOD, CALUMET, BARON NAIRN. She was informed that ROYAL SCOTSMAN should have already arrived at Gironde.

BEAGLE reported (2320) that Gironde was closed owing to Magnetic mines. It was imperative to release French and neutral shipping with troops and important stores. The L/L trawlers sent to Gironde could not be found, and BEAGLE requested immediate replacements.

BERKLEY reported (2330) that, assuming the transports arrived in daylight, embarkation at Pointe de Grave had been arranged with the Polish Liaison Officer to commence at 0700/22, and embarkation from the pier at 1230. The Captain of the port had no knowledge of any French troops for embarkation. There were 40 English nurses for embarkation at Bordeaux. The French had reported that 6 parachutists had dropped in the river above Le Verdon at 1800 and were suspected of laying mines

ORMONDE was ordered (2346) to proceed to Le Verdon.

The French ship PARIS reported that the tugs ABEILLE 8 and ABEILLE 22 and the armed patrol vessel HEUREUX were being sailed at 0800/22. These were to attempt the recovering of a 15000 ton uncompletes *(as typed)* French tanker at La Falaise.

June 22

ARANDORA STAR, escorted by RESTIGOUCHE sailed Plymouth (0050).

LORD GREY ordered to return to Plymouth (0023). C.S.2. informed by C. in C. W. A. that LORD GREY reported ROYAL SCOTSMAN off Gironde awaiting orders.

VANQUISHER (0131) reported, reference to C. in C.'s 2155/21, if no troops at La Pallice, intend proceeding direct to Le Verdon and escorting loaded ships to Plymouth. E.T.A. La Pallice 1800.

GEORGETTE instructed (0135) that INVERFORTH (both L/L Trawlers) was to proceed with her.

LURIGTHAN, CITY OF EVANSVILLE & GLOUCESTER CITY to be sailed from the Bristol Channe to Falmouth for orders (0223)

ORMONDE (0225) acknowledged receipt of C. in C.'s 2346/21 off Lizard and requested earliest T.O.A. Le Verdon dawn Sunday. Asked for confirmation. Confirmation and route sent (0519)

Yacht MAID MARION (0330) have 28 refugees on board, arrived Plymouth (0333), with ALDERPOOL carrying approximately 2800 Polish troops and 70 refugees. No food and water on board.

BERKLEY (0415) notified C.S.2. she was proceeding out of harbour to lead transports.

ETTRICK reported (0630) that she was off the entrance to Bayonne and had been informed by the signal station that she was too large to enter. Requested instructions. She was told to remain under way in vicinity and await orders (0831).

s.s. SAXON QUEEN arrived Plymouth (1701) from Guernsey with 76 Coast Lines Staff.

BERKLEY reported (0720) DELIUS, ROYAL SCOTSMAN & CLAN FERGUSON expected to begin embarkation (0815)

French Aux. Fishing vessel DOM MICHEL NOBLETZ arrived (0825) from Ushant carrying 1 British and 7 French refugees, 33 sailors, 7 soldiers. No food. No water on board.

BELGRAVIAN sailed Southampton for Plymouth (0849)

BERKLEY reported (1006) that Port Dunedin, DELIUS & ROYAL SCOTSMAN were sufficient for embarking all Polish troops.

BEAGLE's 2320/21 C.S.2. informed re L/L/ Trawlers INVERFORTH, GEORGETTE & LORD GREY ordered Gironde if fuel permits – should be in Bay of Biscay

BERVIE BRAES & ST. MELANTE en route Plymouth for Bayonne.

C.S.2. ordered VANQUISHER (1106) to sail any ships at La Pallice unescorted when satisfied no longer required there.

VANQUISHER to act as A/S cover for ships entering Gironde.

ROYAL SOVEREIGN, CANTERBURY & PRINCE BAUDOUIN arrived Dartmouth (1126)

VANQUISHER reported (1124) 250 Poles embarked BLAIRNEVIS, no troops remaining. All oil destroyed. French asked to carry out more demolitions.

VANQUISHER & BLAIRNEVIS proceeding Le Verdon.

BERKLEY asked (1126) by C.S.2. to report number of other troops and personnel requiring embarkation. Answerer *(sic)* (1327).

ORANSAY *(sic)* reported (1215) unable to sail owing bomb damage.

Communication re-established with portable W/T set at Bordeaux (1215)

GEORGETTE, INVERFORTH returned Plymouth (1235)

C.S.2. informed Admiralty (1305) of statement by General Sikorski that 4000 Poles were marching from La Rochelle to Le Verdon and should arrive by 0100/23. 10,000 were still at Bayonne or in vicinity and should arrive during the next few days.

R.A. in GALATEA informed British Ambassador in Bordeaux (1515) that if he was unable to embark pm 22nd GALATEA would leave to go elsewhere, and suggested the Bay of St. Jean de Luz

VANQUISHER reported (1401) that she was taking BLAIRNEVIS to investigate report that there were 400 Polish troops at Ile de Yeu.

ETTRICK reported (1430) that there were 2000 British subjects in her vicinity awaiting embarkation, requested instructions.

Trawler STRATHRANNOCK arrived Plymouth (1435)

French S/M CHASER II arrived Plymouth (1545)

VIVA II ordered 1535 to join C.S.2 off Gironde

French destroyer CDT. DUBOC arrived (1800)

Trawlers ERIMO & GEORGETTE sailed for Le Verdon (1805)

CALCUTTA sailed from Portsmouth (1823) to join C.S.2.

VANQUISHER reported (1900) Poles left 21st for South. BLAIRNEVIS and FORGE sailed for Liverpool unescorted. VANQUISHER in position 46. 37. N. 02. 22. W. course 148° 20 knots.

VANQUISHER ordered by C.S.2. (1917) to rendezvous at 0445/23 with convoy of three ships leaving Gironde.

BROOMPARK instructed to proceed Swansea (1921)

BERKLEY informed VANQUISHER (1930) CLAN FERGUSON & ROYAL SCOTSMAN with 4000 Polish troops leaving Le Verdon 2115 for Liverpool. DELIUS following 23rd with 2000.

B.N.L.O. Bordeaux informed by Admiralty (1937) that s.s. FORMEDINE *(FORT MEDINE?)* with valuable cargo of copper and machine tools should be sailed without delay.

C.S.2. and British Ambassador instructed by Admiralty (1953) most undesirable for GALATEA to remain in same locality any longer owing to S/M and air risks. C.S.2. to leave Arcachon immediately.

KONINGIN EMMA arrived Plymouth (2010)

BERKLEY reported to Admiralty (2045) that she was no longer in touch with British Ambassador

R.A. in BEAGLE reported (2210) leaving Bordeaux when Ambassador departs night of 22nd. Will proceed alongside pier DEC-DAMBES to carry out demolition without French permission, moving on to Pauillac when demolition complete.

CALCUTTA ordered by C.S.2.to proceed at 22 knots to 48. 58. N. 02.58. W.

C. in C. W.A. informed Admiralty (2213) that owing to congestion of refugees he intended to instruct C.S.2. that no persons except troops, British Nationals and certain skilled foreign workmen were to be embarked for the U.K. This was believed to be in accordance with French Official policy

C.S.2. informed Admiralty (2248) that 100 British A/C engines in French Air Ministry depot at Bordeaux should be evacuated. Instructions sent to C.S.2. (2356)

s.s. DEAL arrived Plymouth (2300)

B.N.L.O. reported to C.S.2. (2301) that as French had signed armistice he was evacuating France with British Ambassador immediately.

VIVA II ordered by C.S.2. (2316) to proceed to Le Verdon where she would be used as required for escort duties. s.s. MACLAREN *(?)* arrived Plymouth (2359)

June 23

C.S.2 enquired from Admiralty (0005) whether British Ambassador were to travel in GALATEA or CALCUTTA. If in GALATEA he intended transferring flag to CALCUTTA during absence of GALATEA, Admiralty told him (0217) to act as he thought fit.

C.S.2. approved ETTRICKs (1430/22) and asked ship not to sail without escort.

WREN ordered (0027) by C-in-C to proceed with despatch and escort CLAN FERGUSON and ROYAL SCOTSMAN as far as Smalls.

Admiralty requested that all spare ships should be released for other duties (0035).

R.A. in BEAGLE ordered by Admiralty (0039) not to carry out demolitions without French permission, and at (0045) to remain at Bordeaux to deliver two important messages to follow.

FRASER ordered (0115) by C.S.2. to join him immediately.

BERKLEY reported (0155) embarkation of 6000 Poles completed. DELIUS sailing 0800/23. Essential for BEAGLE to return *(?)* fuel short French refusing to permit embarkation without British assistance Polish officers remaining assisting divert Poles to Bayonne. Suggest s.s. BECKENHAM be diverted thither.

S.N.O. St. Jean de Luz reported (0158) 9000 Poles sailed early 21st in SOBEISKI & BATORY.

British refugees embarking in ETTRICK will require close examination as doubtful cases among them. More Poles arriving will be embarked in ARANDORA STAR. At (0650) S.N.O. enquired when ARANDORA STAR might be expected and stated that FRASER had been withdrawn, believed by C.S.2.

ANTRIM COAST arrived Plymouth (0540)

EMPIRE CRUSADER arrived (0610). CROMARTY arrived (0645)

BROKE reported (0707) s.s. CYCLOPS now with him stated no British warship found Gironde Requires instructions.

FRASER ordered by C.S.2. to proceed to ARCACHON with all despatch.

BERKLEY informed C.S.2. that he was remaining at Le Verdon and had ordered DELIUS & BECKENHAM to await further instructions. s.s. KUFRA had arrived.

WREN diverted by C-in-C W.A. to Le Verdon or as required by C.S.2.

R.A. BEAGLE reported (0830) Germans not yet at Royan.

BERKLEY (0845) to C.S.2. am sailing DELIUS unescorted at (0915/23)

BERKLEY signalled to C.S.2. (0915) French authorities report Germans close to Fort at Royan sailing with transport at once.

MACKAY ordered (0920) to proceed with despatch Le Verdon or as ordered by C.S.2.

Reference BROKE's (0707). C.S.2.ordered him to instruct CYCLOPS to proceed St, Jean de Luz.

VANQUISHER reported (1001) hardly sufficient fuel to reach Liverpool. Demolition party on board. Convoy speed 15 knots.

C.S.2. ordered CALCUTTA (1009) to proceed direct to St. Jean de Luz at 25 knots.

C-in-C informed C.S.2. (1012) BELGRAVIAN due Gironde area (2030/23) LYCAON (1100/24)

R.A. in BEAGLE reported (1030) to Admiralty that their (0230/23) and second copy of their 0124/23 were placed in Adl Darlan's hands by him at 0935/23. Darlan now at cabinet meeting. He had placed himself at Darlan's disposal for communications with Admiralty.

R.A.BEAGLE at 1033 reported Admiralty *(Admiral?)* off the port stated that there were 7 U boats believed close to Gironde intercepting traffic to North Africa. Big ships with troops and materials were at quay.

SOBEISKI arrived Plymouth 1045

C.S.2. instructed BERKLEY to send all empty ships to Bayonne. VIVA II to escort if present.

ORMONDE instructed to proceed to Liverpool (1151)

BERKLEY reported (1145) to C.S.2 have ordered BECKENHAM, KUFRA, KELSO, ORMONDE *(see 1151)* to Bayonne. Proceeding with DELIUS as instructed, no sign of VIVA II (At 1420 reported met VIVA II and passed instructions.) Brought down one enemy bomber at Point*(e)* de Grave a.m./22 believed to be a J U 88.

C.S.2. reported (1151) Ambassador and party embarked on H.M.C.S. FRASER (1100) now proceeding to rendezvous at St. Jean de Luz.

C.S.2. informed by C-in-C W.A. (1152) ORMONDE *(!)*, LYCAON ordered U.K. remainder to proceed Bayonne. C.S.2. to sail for U.K. any ships considered to be in excess of requirements.

S.N.O. St. Jean de Luz reported (1045) situation at 1000/23 ETTRICK loaded with 1000 refugees - only ship present. Approximately 3000 collecting. No A/S protection, considered presence of a destroyer as essential. At (1200) he added "am now filling ETTRICK to capacity by embarking 300 Poles. When may we expect another ship"

C-in-C W.A. (1207) instructed BELGRAVIAN, BARON NAIRN, BARON KINNARD, KERMA to proceed Bayonne.

NOIC Falmouth reported (1318) refugees landed to date: 20th June 2495, 21st June 899, 22nd June 1538 Total 4932 expected to land 600 more 23rd.

Admiralty instructed S.N.O. St. Jean de Luz (1327) to contact Capitaine Bicheloune re important evacuation of 30 French Officers and officials.

French S/M LA CREOLE in tow of French tug ABEILLE 21 reported off Minches (1350)

R.A. BEAGLE instructed (1406) endeavour obtain copy armistice terms, particularly Naval.

CALCUTTA ordered by C.S.2. to proceed at 20 knots (1434)

C.S.2. instructed BEAGLE (1515) to proceed to St. Jean de Luz when present operations completed. C-in-C W.A. informed Admiralty (1523) that it was understood that 49000 *(!)* troops still required evacuation.

BROKE (1601) reported having ordered CYCLOPS to Bayonne proceeding with HARVESTER to Gironde.

BEAGLE reported (1714) no satisfactory answer from Admiral Darlan obtainable. French authorities promise Le TRAIT will be sailed 23rd. FORMEDIDE reported in Le Verdon, will try to sail her for England. The special cases mentioned in Admy's 1416/21 *(?)* all on board BEAGLE and sailed in s.s. SWIFT 15th June. *(?)* 17 evacuees on board C.S.2. to R.A. in BEAGLE (1841). If LE TRAIT & FORMEDINE can be sailed, BEAGLE to escort, if not required remain Bordeaux. If so required WREN to be detailed.

VIVA II ordered by C.S.2. (1843) on arrival Bayonne proceed St. Jean de Luz with any present.

MACKAY ordered by C.S.2. (1846) to St. Jean de Luz.

Admiralty asked R.A in BEAGLE whether demolitions were carried out. (1852)

VANQUISHER reported (1910) weather prevents he *(her?)* doing more than 9 knots. Convoy sent on to Liverpool. VANQUISHER returning Plymouth.

S.N.O. St. Jean de Luz (1940) reported positions at 1900. Remain to be embarked. Poles 1000 plus about 2000 airman. French possible 2500 airmen and 750 experts Czechs about 3000 (later amended to 20).

ETTRICK full to capacity. No further shipping arrived.

HARVESTER ordered (1944) to proceed towards Bayonne and act under orders of C.S.2.

VANQUISHER instructed to continue escort as far as Smalls. Fuel at Milford Haven, then return Plymouth.

WREN to act as A/S patrol on a line 250° from Gironde Whistle Buoy

C. in C, W.A. informed C.S.2. (2029) of report that there was a number of foreign merchant ships off the coast in his area. He was to be prepared to send them into British ports when ordered and to report if he required any additional personnel for armed guards.

BATORY arrived Plymouth (2045)

BEAGLE requested (2034) confirmation of C.S.2's order to proceed to St. Jean de Luz, observing that he was overcrowded with refugees and military parties.

BROKE informed C.S.2. (2058) that HARVESTER was proceeding St. Jean de Luz, but BROKE to Plymouth owing to fuel shortage.

Reference Admiralty's (1852) R.A. BEAGLE reported 2117 that charges were about to be laid when Admiralty's 0039/23 was received. Guard and Oil Staff were told, and believed, that British were after enemy parachute troops.

C.S.2. reported (2223) flag transferred temporarily to CALCUTTA at 2300/23.

June 24

C. in C. W.A. asked C.S.2. (0028) to reply to BEAGLE's 2034/23 re calling at St. Jean de Luz and at (0034) C.S.2. ordered BEAGLE to return to U.K.

C.S.2. ordered VANQUISHER (0125) to proceed with all despatch to 44. 36. N. 01. 19. W. to carry out A/S sweep.

H.M.S. GALATEA with H.M. Ambassador and Canadian and South African Ministers and Staff left St. Jean de Luz for Plymouth.

Admiralty instructed S.N.O. St. Jean de Luz to afford facilities for passage to the U.K. of a number of distinguished Spanish personages and any important nationals of other states if they so desired.

VANQUISHER reported (0347) estimated position of convoy (CLAN FERGUSON & ROYAL SCOTSMAN) at 0400 as 49. 43. N. 05. 55. W.

VANQUISHER (0432) replied to C.S.2.'s (0125) that as he had insufficient fuel to carry out patrol he was remaining with the convoy.

S.N.O. St. Jean de Luz reported (0820) position at Port (0800/24). All embarkation ceased 2100/23, owing to swell. Restarted 0700/24 with ARANDORA STAR inside breakwater. Latest figures appear to be 5000 Poles including airmen, remainder as in 1940/23. At (0925) he added ARANDORA STAR was being filled with Polish Army & Air Force and a few British refugees still arriving. Polish forces will require close scrutiny.

VANQUISHER reported (0835) he had on board V.A. Hallett, Cdr. Sharbrook, 4 R.N.V.R. Sub/Lts. and 60 Naval Ratings demolition party. 2 French Naval Officers and 5 tons demolition stores.

ORMONDE reported (0951) that she was being attacked by A/C and at (0954) that attack has ceased.

C.S.2. instructed BROKE to proceed to St. Jean de Luz and asked what were his orders.

VANQUISHER arrived Plymouth (1000)

BERKLEY reported (1020) that he had insufficient fuel to continue escort of DELIUS beyond 48.26 N. 06.05 W. where he expected to arrive (2130). Intended to return Plymouth and requested relief escort.

S.N.O. St. Jean de Luz (1035) reference C, in C, W.A.'s 1213/23 stated it was proving quite impossible to differentiate persons embarked.

C.S.2. asked (1007) that BERKLEY, VANQUISHER & BROKE or BEAGLE should proceed St. Jean de Luz, after oiling. Two destroyers needed as A/S patrol.

Admiralty informed by HAREBELL (1054) that BEAGLE considered important the destruction of oil installation at Pauillac.

BROKE instructed (1117) to close ORMONDE; BELGRAVIAN, bound for St. Jean de Luz reported (1245) that she had been attacked by U boat, but at (1311) that attack had failed and ceased.

WREN ordered by C.S.2. (1220) to join him at St. Jean de Luz.

D.S.T.O. Falmouth ordered (1221) to sail CITY OF EVANSVILLE, LURIGETHAN, & GLOUCESTER CITY for Bayonne.

D.S.T.O. Plymouth ordered (1247) to sail BAHARISTAN, & JOHN L HOLT to Bayonne.

S.N.O. St. Jean de Luz reported (1315) situation at 1330, approximately 3000 Poles and a number of British refugees embarked on ARANDORA STAR. Number to be yet embarked appears considerable. French airmen not arrived yet. Weather renders impossible embarkation outside the breakwater.

BEAGLE instructed (1324) to close BELGRAVIAN, but reported (1901) no sign of her *(BELGRAVIAN arrived St. Jean de Luz later)*

Ten armed guards ordered (1326) to be in HIGHLANDER by (1600/24)

S.N.O. St. Jean de Luz reported (1430). Poles embarked 2600 remaining CLAN ROSS attacked by A/C (1344) 30 miles N.N.W. of St. Jean de Luz.

Signal (1247) to D.S.T.O. Plymouth re sailing BAHIRISTAN, JOHN L. HOLT, and (1221) to D.S.T.O. Falmouth re sailing EVANSVILLE, GLOUCESTER CITY & LURIGETHAN to Bayonne cancelled.

HIGHLANDER sailed with armed guards (1815)

BEAGLE reported (1905) E.T.A. Plymouth 0650/25 Carrying 44 military personnel and gear, 38 Naval personnel, demolition stores, 15 tons valuable Government stores. One stretcher case, one wounded Officer, one doubtful escaped British prisoner, two German labour corps and three ladies - require identification.

ETTRICK carrying about 1100 British refugees. ARANDORA STAR as previously reported. Escorted by HARVESTER. ETTRICK ordered to Falmouth. ARANDORA STAR to Liverpool.

GALATEA reported (1948) carrying in addition to Embassy Staff, 1 Flight Lt. R.A.F., 1 Lt, ex French Air Force, 1 Lt. R.N.V.R., 1 Air Ministry Official, 5 R.A.F. ranks, 4 army ranks. Wounded:- 1 army Officer, 3 ranks, 1 R.A.F. rank, 14 bags valuables for Polish Finance Minister.

GALATEA arrived Plymouth (2056)

C.S.2. reported (2144) re C. in C.'s 2356/22., refusing permission to embark wives and families causing difficulties and heartrending scenes. S.N.O. asking if he can promise embarkation after priority commitments fulfilled. Impossible to be sure of identity. Understood approximately 2000 womenfolk embarked in BATORY & SOBIESKI. *(KUFRA rammed by SAN DIEGO and sunk in Bay of Biscay 24th)*

June 25

S.N.O. St. Jean de Luz asked by C. in C. (0036) whether following had been embarked:-

      (a)   Colonel Bonavita, 2000 French troops and skilled workmen.

      (b)   Mr. Delaraine and 20 R.D.F. technicians.

      (c)   Captain Bichilone and 30 French Officers and officials.

      (d)   750 French experts, 2000 Polish airmen and 20 Czechs.

      (e)   Number of Spanish personages.

      (f)   Colonel de Gaulles' party.

replied (0858) none arrived. All French parties refused permission owing to armistice.

Sailed from Plymouth for Dartmouth 0330 ST.*(?)* BAHARISTAN, CITY OF LANCASTER, ROBERT L.HOLT, JOHN HOLT.

BROKE arrived Plymouth (0630), BEAGLE (0725), s.s. BALFE (0833).

C.S.2. instructed by C. in C. (0731) that wives and families of Polish soldiers could be embarked if accommodation available.

BERKLEY arrived 0942 bringing 2 British, 4 French soldiers and 3 Australian Labour Corps.

BEAGLE asked (0938) for a list of French ships seen going up Gironde. Reported (1030), 16 French, 2 Dutch and 1 Greek.

French ship DE LA SALLE reported (1130) to Admiral Plymouth that she was making slowly for the mouth of the Gironde under escort. Situation serious. This was passed to C.S.2.

IMOGEN sailed (1220) escorting KONINGIN EMMA & PRINCESS BEATRIX to Milford and STRATHAIRD to Liverpool.

Admiralty informed by C. in C. (1309) that force (of destroyers) was to be prepared to destroy oil stores in Gironde river, and at (1401) that the operation would proceed but that French shipping was not to be interfered with inside territorial waters.

Sailed from St. Jean de Luz (1430) KELSO, BARON KINNARD with 2000 troops for Liverpool.

BARON NAIRN with British refugees and 1200 Polish troops for Falmouth escorted by WREN at 8 knots.

L/L Trawlers BERVIE BRAES and ST. MELANTE sailed for Plymouth (1510).

C.S.2. reported (1525) sailed for Falmouth (1345) empty transports CYCLOPS, KERMA, CLAN ROSS, GLENAFFRIC, BELGRAVIAN, BECKENHAM, escorted by MACKAY and VIVA II at 8 knots.

C-in-C informed Admiralty (1721) that it was intended to release merchant ships reserved for "Aerial" as no further requirement could be foreseen.

HARVESTER instructed (1926) to divert ETTRICK to Plymouth. With reference to s.s. DE LA SALLE (see 1130/25). C.S.2. reported his position, course and speed at (1750) and stated that he could not hope to intercept her unless she broke down. He enquired if Admiralty instruction (1401) re territorial waters applied and was informed (2006) that it did.

Admiralty instructed C-in-C to sail ULSTER PRINCE to embark 1600 British evacuees from Lisbon if she could maintain 18 knots out and home.

C.S.2. ordered RESTIGOUCHE (2325) to sink after part of FRASER as soon as all survivors had been recovered.

June 26

IMOGEN with STRATHAIRD arrived Liverpool (1014).

RESTIGOUCHE reported (1645) that she had on board Captain Allen R.N., 13 Officers and 104 ratings from H.M.C.S. FRASER, 6 ratings from CALCUTTA, 2 R.E. Officers and 24 O.R. R.E.2 Polish Generals, 12 Officers and men. Refugees:- 6 British, 1 French, 1 Spanish, 3 Polish from St. Jean de Luz N.O.I/C Falmouth reported (1719) that ships were overcrowded there with French ratings and small parties were still arriving.

ETTRICK arrived Plymouth (1716)

RESTIGOUCHE arrived Plymouth (1715)

153

C.S.2. reported (2105) CALCUTTA E.T.A. 0845/27., with 3 Officers and 30 ratings (8 injured), survivors from H.M.C.S. Fraser. Wreckage to be lifted from forecastle and only one bower anchor left, which may be fractured.

June 27

ARANDORA STAR & HARVESTER arrived Liverpool 0735.

HIGHLANDER arrived 0930 and CALCUTTA 0932.

WREN instructed (1012) to detach BARON NAIRN to Plymouth and escort KELSO & BARON KINNARD to Liverpool. Reported (2200) detaching BARON NAIRN now E.T.A. 1000/28.

June 28

L/L Trawlers ST.MALANTE, BERVIE BRAES, arrived Plymouth (0724)

BARON NAIRN arrived 0735 with refugees from St. Jean de Luz and anchored Cawsand Bay.

Small French fishing boat with 12 male refugees also arrived Cawsand 0750.

CANTERBURY, ROYAL SOVEREIGN & PRINCE BAUDOIUN (latter with Armed Guard) sailed Dartmouth for Southampton.

Index

Darlan, 174

Dautry, 34, 56, 120, 121

De Beers., 6

De Gaulle, 35, 164

De Haan, 31

Delfin II, 76

Delius, 72, 73

Denholm, 1, 2, 37, 41, 98, 99, 112, 122

deuterium oxide, 4, 6, 33, 34, 116, 119, 123

Deuxième Bureau, 33

Deyczakowski, 76

Diamant club, 24

diamantaires, 6, 24, 32

Diamond Corporation, 61, 63, 64, 68, 69, 124

diamonds, 5, 7, 22, 23, 24, 28, 29, 30, 31, 50, 51, 53, 57, 61, 69, 110, 122, 123

Director of Naval Intelligence, 93

Director of Operations, 56

Director of Scientific Research, 16, 55

Dom Michel Nobletz, 78

Dr Gough, 15, 51, 64

Drax, 96

Dunkirk, 7, 70, 71, 82

Dutch, 10, 80, 81, 150, 160, 161, 167, 179

Dutch gold, 103

Earl, 3, 8, 9, 13, 15, 16, 20, 26, 40, 50, 51, 52, 53, 58, 61, 84, 85, 86, 87, 88, 113

Earlspark, 1

Edinburgh University, 14

Eileen Beryl Morden, 3, 13, 84, 86

Embassy, 28, 40, 42, 68, 77, 92, 125, 129, 156, 160, 168, 178

Emile Bertin French cruiser, 106

Empire, 5, 39, 45, 98

Empire Liberty, 39

Enemy Alien, 92

England, 9, 18, 29, 35, 45, 66, 74, 106, 127, 129, 130, 134, 175

English, 8, 93, 131, 132, 169

Erith, 84, 85

Estreicher Dr Karol, 106

Ettrick, 73, 74, 77, 81, 94

Europe, 81, 92

Evans, 28

Experimental Van, 102

Fal, 10, 49

Falmouth, 9, 49, 50, 52, 53, 56, 58, 64, 72, 74, 76, 82, 123, 125, 137, 142, 144, 146, 147, 148, 149, 150, 152, 153, 154, 155, 156, 157, 158, 159, 160, 162, 165, 166, 167, 168, 170, 175, 177, 178, 179, 180

Fédération des Bourses Diamantaires, 29

Feller & Co, 71, 162

Fifth Column, 80

fifth columnists, 41, 62

Find a Grave, 87

First Sea Lord, 56, 99

First World War, 45

Fleming, Ian 93, 94, 95, 96

Formedine, 72

Fort de France, 106

Fort Medine, 72

France, 1, 3, 5, 7, 13, 16, 17, 23, 25, 27, 28, 29, 30, 31, 34, 41, 49, 54, 56, 57, 62, 64, 67, 70, 71, 72, 87, 91, 94, 99, 110,

160

38515799R00098

Printed in Poland
by Amazon Fulfillment
Poland Sp. z o.o., Wrocław